D1261744

No Longer Property of
Fr. Leonard Alvey Library
Brescia University

Acknowledgments

Many people and organizations offered advice, encouragement, support, and assistance in the realization of this book. The greatest thanks are due to John Finney, who generously invited us time and again to stay at his home in Newport. He was especially helpful in tracking down needed information and keeping our spirits high with amusing anecdotes about his beloved hometown. We are also grateful to Mrs. John Slocum for entertaining us on several occasions and putting us in contact with a number of encouraging local characters. The Redwood Library was a haven for quiet research. We would like to thank the staff there, especially Kay Atkins who graciously found endless sources for our use. The Newport Historical Society, The Newport Preservation Society, and The Newport Restoration Foundation were all extremely cooperative. Richard Grosvenor and John Cherol kindly offered professional advice. Felix de Welden, a great raconteur, gave us memorable insights into the town and was extremely enjoyable company. We would also like to thank Ian Irvine, Catherine Finney, Amanda Aspinall. Stephen Parker, Reily McDonald, Christina Angel, Marie Beebe, Walter J. Whitely, Sister Mary Smith, and Jenine Gordon for helping with the research, and Robert Janjigian for his tireless editorial support.

Introduction

Robert A. M. Stern

Roberto Schezen's photographs convey a powerful sense of Newport's mood and character as a uniquely American place. Through Schezen's lens we see an architecture, evolved over three centuries, as a totality, as though we had visited Newport on one moody autumnal day—as though, for just once, the tourists were gone and the doors of all the houses had swung open for us. As a foreigner to American culture and as an artist, Schezen successfully avoids being trapped by a singular view of Newport, either as a restored Colonial city frozen in time or as society's playground, a place dominated by the values of a few arrogant but not necessarily trivial socialites who built European-inspired palaces along Bellevue Avenue. Schezen permits us to see Newport whole; he liberates its buildings from their historical context, freeing them for the moment of the sometimes glorious, sometimes vainglorious, culture that made it all happen, freeing them to be viewed anew, as form.

Schezen's photographs constitute a wonderful complement to the pioneering work of historians Antoinette Downing and Vincent Scully, authors of *The Architectural Heritage of Newport, Rhode Island.* First published in 1952 and revised in 1967, Downing and Scully's book remains the definitive architectural study on the subject. But its illustrations, many of them merely documentary, do not necessarily live up to the quality of the text; with Schezen's photographs, we are able to see vividly just how remarkable a phenomenon of nature, artistic tradition, and invention this stretch of shore really is.

Newport as we know it is a microcosm of modern urbanism without the intrusion of the industrial city. Seventeenth- and eighteenth-century craftsmen built an extremely coherent and viable city by adapting the forms they knew from England to the demands of the economy and materials of the New World, creating a uniquely American vernacular in what was clearly becoming a key port of trade in the British Empire. The taut clapboard building envelopes, the mullioned windows pushed out as nearly flush to the exterior wall as possible, the gable and gambrel roofs, and the additive compositions that evolved over time—particularly the long, shingled slopes of roof at the rear of buildings—early on established a fluid vocabulary of form, of wall and roof melding together as one continuous skinlike surface, with main mass and lean-to, that has been a hallmark of our domestic architecture.

British occupation during the Revolutionary War devastated Newport's economy, and it was not until just before the Civil War that it would regain a place in the national arena, this time as a leading summer resort. With hotel accommodations at Newport scarce, summer visitors built inexpensive structures intended to last for only one or two seasons. But by the 1850s permanent houses began to be built. In the post–Civil War era,

Newport Houses

Photographs by Roberto Schezen
Text by Jane Mulvagh and Mark A. Weber
Introduction by Robert A.M. Stern

RIZZOLI
NEW YORK

First published in the United States of America in 1989 by
RIZZOLI INTERNATIONAL PUBLICATIONS, INC.
597 Fifth Avenue, New York, NY 10017

Copyright © 1989 Rizzoli International Publications, Inc.
Text copyright © 1989 Jane Mulvagh

All rights reserved.
No part of this publication may be reproduced in any
manner whatsoever without permission in writing from
Rizzoli International Publications, Inc.

Library of Congress Cataloging-in-Publication Data

Schezen, Roberto.
    Newport houses/photographs by Roberto Schezen; text by Jane
Mulvagh and Mark A. Weber; introduction by Robert A.M. Stern.
        p.   cm.
    Bibliography: p.
    ISBN 0-8478-0912-9 :
    1. Architecture, Domestic—Rhode Island—Newport.   2. Mansions-
-Rhode Island—Newport.   3. Architecture and society—Rhode Island-
-Newport.   4. Newport (R.I.)—Buildings, structures, etc.
I. Mulvagh, Jane.   II. Weber, Mark A.   III. Title.
NA7238.N67S34 1989   88-43445
728.8′3′097457—dc19   CIP

Design by Massimo Vignelli
Set in type by David E. Seham Associates Inc., Metuchen, New Jersey
Printed and bound by Dai Nippon Printing, Tokyo, Japan

728.83
S328

Frontispiece: *A view of the Cliff Walk
looking toward Ochre Point on Aquidneck
Island. Originally a footpath providing
fishermen access to the sea, the Cliff Walk
meanders around three miles of rocky
shoreline fronting some of Newport's
grandest cottages, including, from left to
right, The Breakers, Fairholme, and
Anglesea.*

a richer, Northern clientele ushered in a new era in the town's architecture and social life.

Newport was always valued as a beauty spot, but with the coming of the railroads and coastal steamers, it came to be seen as an opportunely located piece of real estate between New York and Boston—a summer suburb for two of America's leading cities. Significantly, the summer colony did not swamp the old city but rather established itself as a suburb of it, beyond the boundaries of the Colonial town, leaving it in a state of benign decrepitude, a state in which it has until only recently remained. As Henry James recalled in 1904, when he revisited the Newport of his youth after a twenty-year-long stay in Europe, old Newport

> . . . had always been so full of treasures of its own as to discredit, from the point of view of taste, any attempt, from without, to stuff it fuller. . . . There remained always a sense, of course, in which the superimpositions, the multiplied excrescences, were a tribute to the value of the place; where no such liberty was ever taken save exactly *because* (as even the most blundering builder would have claimed) it was all so beautiful, so solitary and so "sympathetic."[1]

While no affluent resorters chose to settle in the existing Colonial town, the architects they commissioned, led by Henry Hobson Richardson, were drawn to the architecture of Newport's early buildings as a jumping-off point for a more monumental form of domestic architecture. The resultant flowering of Newport's architecture in the 1880s, labeled by Vincent Scully as the Shingle style, was nothing short of epochal: At last America had found an architectural voice of its own, distinct from others, drawn from native soil, yet part of a wider international culture as well. As Scully has movingly written, the shingled architecture that exemplified Newport's first golden era as a resort

> . . . developed so quickly and richly in the hands of its architects that it must be regarded as having tapped some fundamental items of American belief: in intellectual pluralism, for example, wherein many divergent attitudes and influences are supposed to merge into an integrated but not "exclusive" whole; in cultural democracy, through which artistic meaning is supposed to be extracted from common forms serving everyday needs at modest scale . . . ; in Emersonian nature, "the circumstance which dwarfs every other circumstance," into which the man-made shapes, reflecting "the soul of the Workman" streaming through them, are to "nestle."[2]

The new architecture of the summer colony was ideally suited to fulfill the expansive programs of prosperous resorters. Exuberant and picturesque, it was complex and powerfully original in form. Classical and colloquial, it was the deeply felt expression of architects who were no longer the typical copybook provincials of the 1830s and 1840s but accomplished professionals, well traveled and well schooled in the forms and planning techniques of the grand tradition of French Classicism as well as the charming vernaculars of the Ile de France and Normandy. Their innovation was to harness the grand principles of architectural composition and planning to distinctly native conditions. While the freely composed, picturesque domesticity of the so-called Queen Anne Revival style developing simultaneously in England is related to the Shingle style, the American work is wholly its own in its evocation of the American past. The Shingle-style work of Richardson and his followers has a tautness of surface, a sweeping horizontality, resulting from the simple and direct expression of a wood frame sheathed in a skin of clapboard or shingle. The use of indigenous stone and wood shingles, particularly when the shingles weathered to a dark brownish-gray, suggested a romantic affinity with Newport's rocky bluffs and the gray, sweeping horizontality of sea beyond.

The discovery of America's architectural past was seen as a sign of the nation's cultural coming of age and a way to reaffirm the Union after the divisive Civil War. The Boston architect Robert Swain Peabody wrote in the *American Architect and Building News* in 1877, "With our centennial year have we not discovered that we too have a past worthy of study? . . . our Colonial work is our only native source of antiquarian study and inspiration."[3]

By the century's end it did not seem enough for Americans to come to terms with their national past. Many began to shift their gaze onto the international scene—some, like Henry James, by expatriating themselves, others by undertaking to emulate the European background, if not exactly the reality, of their colonial forefathers. Ogden Goelet, a wealthy New York real estate developer, initiated a change in architectural aspirations with his palatial Ochre Court of 1888. Its evocation of Europe's architectural past ignited a domestic-building explosion in Newport that would last into the present century. It set the era's standard not only for opulence and scale but also for historical authenticity. Goelet's architect, Richard Morris Hunt, designed a free but rather severe interpretation of sixteenty-century French Renaissance elements, which he would later bring to an apogee in North Carolina at Biltmore.

As Newport reached a frenzy of frivolity around 1900, it fascinated—and appalled—many Americans, who viewed it as a modern-day Babylon. Henry James found that the town, which he had described in 1870 as "a series of organized homes" forming a "really substantial and civilized"[4] resort community, had been completely transformed. "What an idea . . . ," he wrote, "to have seen the miniature spot of earth . . . as a mere breeding ground for white elephants! They look queer and conscious and lumpish—some of them, as with an air of the brandished proboscis, really grotesque . . . . "⁵ For James, even nature had been corrupted by wealth; at Newport, one could hear "something like the chink of money itself in the murmur of the breezy little waves."⁶

James notwithstanding, Newport's palaces cannot be dismissed as a near-ridiculous dream of a would-be American aristocracy. True, these palaces were extravagant, and they were self-indulgent, but they were in their way sincere in their celebration of the newly minted wealth of the world's leading industrial society. And they were not without a sense of noblesse oblige—a respect for what went before and the good sense to leave it—the old town, that is—alone.

The fanciful dream that Newport's families shared was shared by many, rich and poor alike, and in a way represents the essence of the American dream: that from modest circumstances, fortunes can be made, enjoyed, even flaunted. If the Shingle style created out of the nation's Colonial past a mythic prehistory, the palace-building era claimed the new democracy's ability to achieve a material environment, and perhaps even a culture, as refined as that of Europe.

Newport's great palaces offer many lessons, not the least of which are those of craft. Built quickly, they were not built carelessly; over the course of a single decade they raised the level of American building to the highest it had ever been. Realized through the evolving talents of Hunt, McKim, Mead and White, and Horace Trumbauer, the palaces also brought with them another lesson: the lesson of the land. They represent the first significant American attempt to create an integrative architecture of buildings and land since the time of Jefferson. Not just behemoths rootlessly afloat in a sea of turf, most of these palaces meet their sites with a carefully arranged substructure of loggias, terraces, parterres, and lavish gardens. They are great architectural machines fully imbued with a strict sense of landscape as structured form.

Ironically, Newport's great mansions, though frequently larger and always more extravagant and better equipped than the European palaces and chateaux they emulated, did not preside over vast land holdings but commanded lots only marginally bigger than those in many affluent suburbs. So even in its palace-building era, Newport was just a suburb. And for all its opulence and pretensions, for all the effort to deny the national context, it remained essentially democratic: Running along the rocky shoreline, just beyond some of the most extravagant mansions, the narrow public pathway, Cliff Walk, permitted the masses to enjoy not only dramatic ocean vistas but views of the great houses as well.

For most of us today, a visit to Newport is confined to the palaces, the "white elephants" miraculously preserved for us to gawk at, to momentarily share an aristocratic fantasy as we marvel at the luxury and gasp. Sadly, few tourists get to see the simpler Shingle-style houses of the 1880s, precisely because so many of them still function as private residences; so suited are they to the basic American way of life that they continue to be valued as places to live in. So suitable, even comfortable, are these houses that for a long time they ceased to be regarded as architecture at all—just fine building, a vernacular. It was not until the 1950s, when Scully interpreted these works for architects and the general public, that we came to recognize their deeper meanings and even to value them as models for the architecture of our own time.

As a student at Yale University, where I was privileged to study with Scully, I came to realize that these Shingle-style houses were what I admired most about American architecture, that they were not just fine buildings but architecture with a capital A. Inspired by Scully, I began to see a noble side to American culture that I had not quite before imagined and began to sense a direction I would pursue as an architect. Many other architects were also inspired by Scully's vision so that now, in the "postmodern" era, architects and planners—who once again see the American present as a function of its complex and not necessarily ideal past—once again willingly enter into a dialogue with history in order to structure contemporary form in relation to the enduring values of our largely self-invented culture. Through our reinterpretation of the Shingle style and beyond, through our acceptance of the cultural and formal continuities that Newport as a whole represents, a contemporary approach to architecture has emerged that builds upon the past as it speaks to our own age.

Notes

1. Henry James, *The American Scene*, ed. Leon Edel (Bloomington, Ind.: Indiana University Press, 1968), 211–12; originally published by Chapman and Hall Ltd., London, 1907.

2. Vincent Scully, *The Shingle Style Today or The Historian's Revenge* (New York: George Braziller, 1974), 9.

3. Robert Swain Peabody, "Georgian Homes of New England," *American Architect and Building News* 2 (October 20, 1877): 338–39.

4. Henry James, *The Nation* 272 (September 15, 1870): 170–72.

5. James, *The American Scene*, 224.

6. Henry James, *The Ivory Tower* (Fairfield, Conn.: Augustus M. Kelley, 1976, Scribner's Reprint Series), 23; originally published by Charles Scribner & Sons, New York, 1917.

The island is pleasantly laid out in hills and vales and rising ground; hath plenty of excellent springs, and fine rivulets, and many delightful landscapes of rocks, promontories, and adjacent lands . . . very pretty and pleasantly sited . . .
Bishop Berkeley, 1729

Above: *The Erastus Pease House of 1785 has a Dutch gambrel roof with curved, upswept eaves.*

Opposite: *Lower Pelham Street is located in the heart of Newport's restored eighteenth-century Hill District.*

Above: *Classical triangular pediments were used to decorate mid-eighteenth-century, Georgian-style doorways.*

Above: *Carried by fluted Doric pilasters,*
a dentil-trimmed pediment surmounts an
Adam-period fanlight window.

Above: *Carved gravestones mark the resting places of the Arnold Burial Ground on Pelham Street.*

Opposite: *Bellevue Avenue, the tree-lined corridor developed in the 1850s, was the address of choice for the socially ambitious.*

Newport: In Perspective

We are not in America. We are in a little extra-territorial province that is more class-conscious than Versailles.
Theophilus North, *Thornton Wilder*

As one journeys through the facts and fables of Newport's rich history, one is unwittingly taken full circle: from the ideological struggle of its first seventeenth-century settlers, who sought religious tolerance, through the feats of the American revolutionaries, who rid themselves of "Old World" notions and dependencies, and back to the imitative antics of the late-nineteenth-century resort socialites, who embraced and copied the architectural settings, modes, and manners of Europe.

Civic and individual pride in the buildings of this town have effected, over four centuries, a consistent architectural integrity. Whether the buildings were erected as statements of religious freedom, such as the Touro Synagogue—the first in America—or as bold tributes to personal fortune, such as William K. Vanderbilt's Marble House, each adds to Newport's architectural and historic pride.

Rather than writing only about the architectural styles derived from the specific fashionable forms and structural possibilities of each period, it is interesting, for a change, to investigate as well the motives of those who commissioned them: their tastes, social positions, physical requirements, and financial limitations. Newport is a town whose buildings can be described in the light of their owners' characters and aspirations; for both the buildings and the documentation have survived, carefully preserved by the local inhabitants.

Thornton Wilder identified nine distinct cities within Newport in his book, *Theophilus North,* which was set in 1926, at the close of the Gilded Age. The first was the seventeenth-century town of the earliest settlers; the second, the more affluent eighteenth-century city in which the advocates and enemies of independence lived behind handsome Greek Revival doorways; the third was the docks and wharves along the waterfront from which the prosperous merchants traded. The army and naval forces had their own city, as did the nineteenth-century intellectuals. The gargantuan palaces erected along the coastline by the nineteenth-century socialites formed another city, set apart and waited on by the residents of the seventh city: the servants tucked away in modest quarters behind the grand avenues. A "city" of hotels and guest houses provided temporary abodes for the camp followers and attendant journalists, while within their genteel homes a thriving middle class lived, ignoring the pastimes of the ostentatious resorters. The inhabitants of each city erected their own buildings, which clearly reflected their life-styles.

The story of Newport crystalizes the essence of American history. Set on the southern tip of Rhode Island, at the mouth of Narragansett Bay, it was one of the first settlements founded on the notions of religious and political tolerance, which became the backbone of American political thinking. From Newport's harbor sailed the revolutionary fleets that fought for these rights. The town also boasts the first Quaker Meeting House in the United States. The flowering of an internationally acclaimed American literary reputation germinated here and included such luminaries as Henry James, Henry Wadsworth Longfellow, and Edith Wharton. And as America emerged as the leading industrial nation in the late nineteenth century, so its robber barons, who had created this wealth, arrived in what was to become the most fashionable summer resort in the New World.

There is probably no area in America that is more specifically identified with the early history of the nation. The original, endemic population of Rhode Island, the Red Indians, christened the area *Aquidneck*, meaning "Isle of Peace." The island is fourteen miles long and is washed by the warm Gulf Stream. *Pocasset,* later called Portsmouth, on the upper side of the island, was where the first whites settled in 1638. Eager to rid themselves of the Indian association, which posed a constant threat, these settlers renamed the area Rhode Island around 1644.

Newport, the largest town on the island, was settled between Marlborough and Tanner streets in 1639. This site offered an attractive climate and soil, a natural harbor, and an independent outpost for those who had suffered from the religious persecution of the Puritan and Pilgrim settlers in New York and Massachusetts. It was settled by William Coddington, the first governor of the colony, William Brenton, John Clarke, Thomas Hazard, Henry Bull, and William Dyer. These men and their families had been forced out of Massachusetts because of their religious beliefs and, led by Roger Williams, whom they met on the way, they purchased the area from the Indians for some wampum and a few brass buttons.

The sea had a very strong influence on Newport, constantly reminding one of its sweeping force as it advances and retreats in and out of the harbor and coves with breaker force. By day, walk a mile or two in either direction and confront its defining limits; by night, lie listening to the fog horns, warning through the Atlantic mists. The smell of the sea air, the wail of the wind, the salt on your face—the senses cannot avoid acknowledging the ocean's presence. It is the single most important element in the town's evolution.

The sea has a very strong influence on Newport, constantly reminding one of its sweeping force as it advances and retreats in and out of the harbor and coves with breaker force. By day, walk a mile or two in either direction and confront its defining limits; by night, lie listening to the fog horns, warning through the Atlantic mists. The smell of the sea air, the wail of the wind, the salt on your face—the senses cannot avoid acknowledging the ocean's presence. It is the single most important element in the town's evolution.

The sea has always determined the livelihood of Newporters, and

the first buildings—homes, wharves, and warehouses—were erected around the harbor. The streets were laid out, as in many American cities, on a grid system, following the teachings of Marcus Vitruvius Pollio, the Roman architect. Vitruvius believed that a study of the prevailing winds and cross currents should be made of a site, with streets designed on a grid to ensure maximum air circulation, giving a city "lungs." According to historian Antoinette Downing, Newport was never an overcrowded town. The buildings were well spaced, as there was enough land and timber both to build and to heat them.

Newport's harbor was a key to the town's early success, as well as the American nation's eventual independence. The natural harbor encouraged the establishment of "triangular trading": Shiploads of molasses were imported from plantations in Jamaica, converted into rum in Newport's factories, and shipped to Africa, where the rum was traded for slaves destined for work on American plantations. Many British colonies were supplied with goods manufactured in Newport and exported through its harbor. During the American Revolution, Newport played a crucial part in the British defeat. With the aid of the French fleet, naval attacks were launched from Newport, aiding in the final success of the revolutionaries. Similarly, during the American Civil War, Newport's naval role was vital. Indeed, a naval presence remained at Newport until 1973, when the United States Navy moved its base down the Atlantic coast to Virginia.

By the mid-eighteenth century, the population of thriving Newport had reached 12,000, supported by trade and manufacturing—notably three sugar refineries, seventeen sperm-oil and candle factories, and twenty-two rum distilleries.

Aside from the humanitarianism it fostered, the town benefited materially from its policy of religious freedom, for in encouraging the settlement of Jews and Quakers, known for their hard work and business acumen, Newport developed as a trading center, rivaling both Boston and New York in the eighteenth century. The Quakers had put down roots by 1656, and a deed dated 1677 granted Jewish burial rights on a site that is now the Jewish cemetery. A century later, rich and eminent Jews arrived, largely from Portugal and the West Indies, and an established Jewish community developed.

Enterprise built the town. The arrival of the Portuguese Jews in 1656 was crucial to this mercantile growth as the life of Aaron Lopez, who participated in the triangular trade, demonstrates. Following in his half-brother's footsteps, he arrived in Newport, fleeing persecution in Portugal, where his family had lived secretly as Jews. His trading started on a very modest scale— between Newport and Providence—but by 1767 he was doing business with the West Indies and eventually with Bristol, England, supplying lumber in exchange for dry goods and

89934

728.83
S328

Brescia College Library
Owensboro, Kentucky
19

hardware. Lopez was canny enough to understand that eighteenth-century trade was unstable, so he diversified. By the eve of the Revolution he owned thirty trading ships, which were moving various goods between the British Isles, the West Indies, and the east coast of America. By 1774, however, Newport was in commercial decline because of the devastating effects of the Revolution, and Lopez left to operate elsewhere.

The influx of ambitious and pioneering folk created a wealthy, cosmopolitan environment. Newport was soon recognized not only as a major trading and manufacturing town, but also as an intellectual center. The Redwood Library and Athenaeum, founded in 1748 and believed to be the oldest American library in continuous existence, and Bishop Berkeley's Philosophical Society provided facilities for the intelligentsia of the town. Visitors interested in philosophical and academic debate were attracted to Newport, and gradually writers and painters took up residence as well, many moving from Boston, Philadelphia, and New York. Seeking to add stature and permanence to their achievements, these men turned to Greek and Roman architectural forms to reflect their knowledge of, and belief in, the classical principles in both architecture and philosophy. The use of columns of the classical order and symetrically balanced, well-proportioned rooms lent dignity and wisdom to their surroundings. In later years, the introduction of Palladian forms promoted a notion of permanence and historical continuity in the town.

As early as 1729 Newport was established as a watering place, for the picturesque seascape ensured its development as a resort. Many have noted how similar in beauty and climate it is to the Mediterranean islands, enjoying, as Bishop Berkeley wrote to Thomas Prior in 1729, "a climate [that] is like that of Italy, and not at all colder in the winter than I have known it everywhere north of Rome. The spring is late, but to make amends they assure me the autumns are the finest and longest in the world, and the summers are much pleasanter than those of Italy by all accounts, for as much as the grass continues green, which it doth not there."

Besides being famous for its summer season, Newport glories in the breathtaking autumns that characterize all of New England. The brilliantly colored trees at the end of autumn seem like redcoats, brave in death, as they bleed into winter. Crimson, vermilion, mustard, and cinnamon-colored leaves fall to the earth, laying a carpet for the incoming dark fogs which shroud the island until early April.

From the early eighteenth century, southerners were attracted to Newport's temperate shores, escaping from the exasperating heat of summer in the South. Tourism had escalated by the 1830s, and the first hotel was opened on Catherine Street in 1825. The Atlantic and Ocean House hotels soon followed. Until the 1850s resorters tended to stay in these hotels in the center of town, but as the influx of summer visitors increased, many decided to build their own houses. Unlike those who stayed in hotels, the owners of summer houses had no "season" and would often spend the entire year in these homes. George Noble Jones was one of the first southerners to build his summer house, Kingscote, on Bellevue Avenue, which overlooked the sea. Erected in 1841, it started the trend for houses along this valuable stretch of land. These first resort houses gloried in their rural surroundings. In order to be in harmony with the treescape, the buildings were constructed of wood, in informal styles, their masses artfully broken up by timbering, reflecting their owners' search for a rural ideal. They were erected partly in reaction to the burgeoning industrialism that prevailed in the large cities and from which their owners were seeking refuge. These were not houses for show but homes in which to enjoy nature's summer delights.

At this time social life was very informal. Time was passed riding up and down First and Second beaches, or competing in archery and croquet competitions. Picnics were enjoyed on the beaches, rocky promontories, or inland riverbanks. Ladies entertained at tea and chocolate parties, as formal dinners were not fashionable until the 1870s. If gentlemen wished to dine together, they sought each other's company at The Reading Room, Newport's exclusive gentleman's club, established in 1854.

Alfred Smith's opportunism acted as a catalyst for extensive real estate development, which began in 1858. While he was working as a tailor in Manhattan, several of his clients inquired about properties in Newport, and he decided to take up a more lucrative trade: buying plots along the seashore to sell to wealthy New York, Boston, and Philadelphia resorters, as well as the many southerners who were already summer residents of the town's hotels. Ocean Drive, which skirts the coastline around Newport, was opened in 1869, extending the stretch along which to build, though the most fashionable still chose to construct their summer homes along Bellevue Avenue.

The relaxed, informal pace of life was to change after the Civil War with the arrival of a very different resorter—the robber baron—who followed in the wake of New York and Boston's social elite, enjoying their "watering-place trivialities," as Edith Wharton called them.

Consequently, by the 1870s Newport's historical significance had shifted. The projects of the architect Richard Morris Hunt over three decades clearly reflect this change: He converted a town of wood into a town of marble. It was no longer a harbor of refuges and outsiders eager to maintain intellectual debate, political dissent, or industrial success. It had become a resort town for those who had achieved significance elsewhere; a seasonal playground for the powerful, rather than the primary home of those with a committed role to play in the local affairs of the town.

Much has been said and written about the Gilded Age. The popular focus on this notorious era has consequently blurred the perspective on the history of this long-established town. One should bear in mind that these tales of the marble "summer cottages" are but a footnote to Newport's complete history. The new resorters, like their predecessors, were drawn to the panoramic views, the temperate climate, the thriving artistic and intellectual communities, and the fascinating history of this old colonial town. Once the New York Yacht Club had won the Americas Cup title from the British, the race was hosted by the Americans at Newport, and a large sailing fraternity was thereby attracted. Newport was conveniently situated between the major conurbations of New York, Boston, and Philadelphia and could be reached either by train and then ferry or by the Fall River steamboat line from New York, aboard the luxury ships *Commonwealth* and *Priscilla*. Women and children spent the summer there while the men would, typically, leave Wall Street on Friday afternoon, board the steamboat in New York harbor, and arrive in time for dinner. A return trip was made on Sunday night. By the late nineteenth century people flocked to the town just because others came, one following another to perform on yet another social stage.

One of the most famous natural attractions of the area was the Cliff Walk, which runs for three and a half miles along the eastern shore of the island. Originally providing a series of landing points for fishermen to moor along its rocky outcrops, this bouldered stretch of Atlantic coastline was soon cherished for its passage from First Beach to beyond Ochre Point (named after the color of the cliffs) in any season. Here, windblown walks could be taken to witness the changing moods of the sea and the shifting skies. It was along this coastline, flanked on the other side by Bellevue Avenue, that the wealthy built their "summer cottages." Henry James, a resident writer, despaired the construction of these houses when he returned in 1904: "White elephants, as one may call them best, all cry and no wool, all house and no garden, make now for three miles, a barely interrupted chain, and I dare say I think of them best, and of the distressful and inevitable waste they represent."

The grandest of these mansions, Ochre Court, Rosecliff, Marble House, and The Breakers, were built during the Gilded Age (1880–1910). Their worldly ornateness stands in senseless, defiant contrast to the natural beauties of the ocean which they overlook and which their owners supposedly came to Newport to enjoy. They call to mind the disfigurement of nature that Des Esseintes, Huysmans' decadent character in *Against Nature,* carried out in pursuit of aesthetic perfection. Like Des Esseintes, who wanted to "dim all contrasts of a brilliant object that would kill everything around it, drowning the gleams of silver in the golden radiance," by gilding and bejeweling the shell of his pet tortoise, so these plutocrats gilded the shore of Newport in an arrogant, or at least foolhardy, attempt to finance the triumph of artifice over nature. At one point the mansion owners tried to have the Cliff Walk closed to ensure their privacy. The townsfolk were appalled but fortunately uncovered an early law that protected free passage to provide the fishermen with access to the shore. Forced to accept this statute, the magnates had to ensure that the walk was safe for the public and some, such as the Astors, constructed terraces that overhung the path so that their houses could not be seen. For this reason some of the Cliff Walk is still tunneled.

Set like rows of telescopes, these houses looked out to the Europe that they struggled to emulate. The new American dynasties that they housed wanted to revive the aristocratic traditions of the Old World and, by association, accord themselves and their achievements the status of New World aristocrats. Their occupants paid homage to the old values of undemocratic and leisured Europe, ignoring the very values that had created America: equality, democracy, and the work ethic.

"Nowhere else in this country—nowhere of course, within the range of our better civilization—does business seem so remote, so vague, and unreal. It is the only place in America in which enjoyment is organized. If there be any poetry in the ignorance of trade and turmoils and the hard processes of fortune, Newport may claim her share of it," observed Henry James. Here even the most pioneering, independent, and self-made magnates became popinjays. They eagerly performed the social dance, with their coquettish women, like marionettes controlled by the powerful social hostesses, Mrs. Astor, Mrs. Stuyvesant Fish, and Mrs. Vanderbilt. The master of ceremonies was Ward McAllister, who had helped Mrs. Astor select the "Four Hundred," the elite, Eastern-dominated list of society families.

Society in Newport could now be compared to that at the court of Versailles, Thornton Wilder's class-conscious "extra-territorial province." As at Versailles, the "season" at Newport was controlled by these society arbiters and was strictly formalized. Fixed for ten weeks in the summer months, attendance was de rigueur if one wished to mix with the fashionable. One was left in doubt as to whether or not one was accepted into society. Indeed, Cleveland Amory recorded in his book *The Last Resorts* that one precondition of entry was a personal fortune of at least $5 million and a "cottage" that cost no less than $1 million. From morning until night the resorters' day was mapped out in a series of pastimes designed to encourage social exchange, conspicuously display both wealth and leisure, and ensure marriages between the "Four Hundred" and the aristocracy of Europe. In one glorious season "The Avenue" boasted three debutantes married off to British aristocrats, the most famous alliance being that between the reluctant Consuelo Vanderbilt and the ninth Duke of Marlborough. Day-to-day life was beset with tricks to catch out the uninitiated. Every afternoon a coach parade took place along Bellevue Avenue, in which families could display their latest carriage or equipage. However, beware those that overtook the carriage of one of a higher social order! Up and down they would go greeting one another heartily when first they passed, with a modest smile on the second occasion, and without acknowledgment on the third.

Side by side along Bellevue Avenue stood replicas of the Grand Trianon, a Genoan palace, Compton Wynyates, and François Premier's castle. These were the settings for society's summer performances. One host, on welcoming a royal European guest to his château, observed, "Well, the château style is not a novelty to you, sir." "No", replied the guest, "but four on one block certainly is!" As the strip of land between the Cliff Walk and Bellevue Avenue, laid out in 1851, was limited, the prices for these plots became astronomical. Consequently, large mansions were built on relatively small tracts of land (between two and ten acres) reflecting not only the scarcity of land but also two characteristics of American life that contrasted vividly with the European tradition. Firstly, the grand European houses which they imitated would have been set in hundreds or thousands of acres of park and farmland, upon which tenant farmer, estate worker, and nobleman all made their living. By contrast, there was no real tradition of the landed estate and its socioeconomic structure in American life. The resorters took these buildings out of their context and placed them on "suburban" plots. Secondly, the close proximity of these huge houses along the shore proclaimed their true purpose: They were built to facilitate the social life of a minute segment of American society and are thus a true record of the American love of neighborliness. The owners sought close contact with each other, to such an extent that one can lean out of the window of a Grand Trianon and call out to one's neighbor in his copy of Compton Wynyates next door. Privacy was not a high priority. Indeed, William K. Vanderbilt erected Marble House at the front of his seaside plot so that it could be more easily admired from the road. Though most of the owners of these properties had traveled extensively on the Continent, their attempts to transpose European culture onto the American way of life were, at the very least, strained. Such imitation confounded Edith Wharton, who wrote in *The Age of Innocence:* "It seems stupid to have discovered America only to make it a copy of another country. . . . Do you suppose Christopher Columbus would have taken all that trouble?"

Umberto Eco, the Italian philosopher, has investigated this curious American lust for the past and for things European. His conclusions can certainly be applied to this segment of Newport's society. In *Travels in Hyperreality* he wrote: "There is a constant in the average American imagination and taste, for which the past must be preserved and celebrated in full-scale authentic copy; a philosophy of immortality as duplication. It dominates the relation with self, with the past, not infrequently with the present, always with history and, even, with European tradition."

Man's arrogance can distort reality; he can fail to grasp the transience of a dynasty, the mortality of man. These houses will stand for but a second in the millenium of history, their dynasties already forgotten, passed to the grave. By the Second World War they had become decaying monoliths gradually being erased by the sea as it ate away at the coastline. Their values were tumbling. Cleveland Amory estimated that the ten largest mansions were worth $2.8 million in 1925; by 1950 their value had plummeted to a mere $823,000. The Crash of 1929 initiated the decline; many could no longer afford to have several summer homes and sold them. Others were crippled by taxation or could no longer find or pay for the numerous servants that were required to keep the houses up. (At the height of the Gilded Age, Mrs. Ogden Mills had boasted that she could hold a dinner for one hundred guests without calling in extra staff!) Furthermore, fashionable society had accepted new players who chose to summer elsewhere, and for a time Newport was abandoned by many.

The houses fell into disrepair or, at best, were converted into schools, such as The Salve Regina College, which was donated by the philanthropic Goelet family. Others became old peoples' homes. The Newport historian, Maude Howe Elliott, recalled her mother's prophecy at the beginning of the century: "It is within the bounds of possibility that Newport may become an educational center. Fashion may go elsewhere, the rich people may tire of their great houses, which could be turned into school and colleges."

More recently, the largest homes have become curiosities to be visited by tourists, who are generally perplexed at the thought of family life taking place in these edifices, which seem more like stage sets than human dwellings. However, for many, unable to travel to Europe, these houses and their contents offer one of the few tangible contacts with the Old World. On arriving in Newport the mansions are the first buildings to which one's attention is drawn.

These mansions, civic buildings, merchant houses, and inns, now carefully restored and curated, offer an invaluable record of American life. Newport and America in general are indebted to the vigorous and undeterred conservationist activities of The Newport Historical Society, The Newport Restoration Foundation, The Preservation Society, and philanthropist Doris Duke. Between them they have ensured that these structures, which housed and serviced a variety of settlers, revolutionaries, traders, intellectuals, painters, and socialites, have been preserved.

The Preservation Society was founded by Mrs. George Henry Warren in 1945 following a delightfully impulsive act of philanthropy; on hearing that the Hunter House was to be sold and knocked down, she and her husband bought it. Having authentically restored the building, they approached their friends in the Newport community to donate or lend original colonial furniture and persuaded many to join the society. Their goal was to preserve the town's heritage, and they were leased The Breakers by The Countess Szechenyi, (née Gladys Vanderbilt) for a mere $1 a year. The Elms was their next acquisition. The society now operates daily tours around the houses and provides informative and entertaining lectures.

With the departure of the navy in 1973, Newport was given a new lease on life. As a quiet, elegant colonial town it attracted a new type of resident who wanted to leave the big-city hubbub and live and work at a slower pace in a town full of handsome buildings, a fascinating history, and attractive countryside. Many small businesses, some catering to the sailing and sporting visitors, grew up. Careful restoration and a thriving service sector, including restaurants, museums, and gift and craft shops, attracted a new resorter—most often a day tourist or sailing enthusiast—to the town.

The misconception of Newport as a faded resort center from a lost era is soon discarded. The social razzmatazz may have gone, particularly with the New York Yacht Club's loss of the Americas Cup in 1984, but a more enduring attraction that has never deserted Newport remains: the indestructible dignity and beauty of a very old, lovingly restored colonial town cared for by residents who live there year-round. These are the people from whom one learns about the true nobility of Newport, who are reflected in its buildings—citizens remembered as political pioneers, such as Samuel Ward; master craftsmen such as the Townsends and Goddards; eminent painters such as Gilbert Stuart, John LaFarge, and William Hunt; the writers James and Wharton; philanthropists like Charles Van Zandt; and architects and intellectuals such as Bishop Berkeley. To gleen their stories takes time; their lights may shine more dimly than the spotlights of the socialites, but they will shine longer, for they illuminate the conscientious progress of man, not his hedonism.

Henry James was relieved that the pleasure seeker had failed to corrupt the enduring charm of Newport. "For this, perhaps, we may thank rather the modest, incorruptible integrity of the Newport landscape than any very intelligent forebearance on the part of the summer colony. The beauty of this landcape is so subtle, so essential, so humble, so little a thing of feature and pretension, that it cunningly eludes the grasp of the destroyer or the reformer, and triumphs in impalpable purity even when it seems to make concessions." (*Portrait of Places*).

The Whitehorse Tavern, 1673

For a man seldom thinks with more earnestness of anything than he does of his supper.
Samuel Johnson

Opposite: *The tavern's gambrel roof and pedimental doorways were eighteenth-century additions by the Nichols family.*

The Whitehorse Tavern, the oldest tavern in America, was granted its first license in 1687 to the proprietor William Mayes, Sr. Situated at the junction of Marlborough and Farwell streets, up the hill from the harbor, it was to shelter an unexpected variety of guests, ranging from earnest Quakers and community-conscious town councillors to notorious pirates and smugglers. William Mayes ran a respectable saloon, but his son, William Jr., was far from a pillar of Newport society. He had gone to sea at an early age and returned in 1699 with a fortune, gained by pirating in the Red Sea. The authorities were determined to hang him, but he proved such a popular figure with the local townsfolk that the official decision was blocked by public demand, and his life was saved. William took over his father's public house and prided himself on providing strong liquor and fast company.

Robert Nichols, who married into the Mayes family, inherited the tavern, which was to remain in his family for 200 years. In 1708 the Town Council, hosted by Nichols, started to meet there, since the Council House had not yet been built, and when Jonathan Nichols II took over the license, the building became a center of civic affairs, as Jonathan was the Lieutenant Governor.

Against the Nichols family's wishes, the tavern harbored British troops during the Revolution. When a British officer arrived requesting room from Walter Nichols, the patron at the time, he resigned himself to the inevitable but not without making a stand. "Take it all, Sir, take it all. Do you think I would permit my family to live under the same roof as British soldiers?" The British were to remain there for three years.

The Whitehorse Tavern continued to be a center of good fare and company until the twentieth century, when it functioned as a run-down boarding-house. Recognizing the historical and architectural merit of the fine clapboard building, The Newport Preservation Society bought it in 1954 and restored it.

Since then the building has been returned to its original role: It has been sold to a restaurateur and is now regarded as one of the best dining houses in Newport.

The Quaker Meeting House, 1699-1700

We meet on the broad pathway of good faith and good will; no advantage shall be taken by either side, and all shall be openness and love.
Treatise with the Indians, *1682, William Penn*

Opposite: *The restored Quaker Meeting House is one of Newport's most significant colonial buildings.*

The first apostles of Quakerism arrived in Newport, from England, in 1657. Fellow Quakers had already suffered persecution in Boston and New York, but Rhode Island prided itself on religious tolerance and was largely a Quaker state.

These Quaker, or Society of Friends, settlers initially met and worshipped in each others' homes, notably those of William Coddington, the first governor of the colony, and Henry Bull. The Friends emphasized and lived by their belief in religious freedom and discussion, tolerance of the Jew and the Indian, and equal rights for women. Indeed, women were encouraged to hold separate meetings to discuss issues and business so that they did not rely entirely on their menfolk and thereby developed a greater sense of independence.

By 1672 Newport had become such a distinguished center of Quakerism in America that the founder of The Society of Friends, the Englishman George Fox, paid a visit to the community. It was he who instilled in his followers the belief that man should return to a simpler form of worship, more closely related to the edicts of early Christianity. This simplicity and directness were to characterize not only the style of worship but also the very buildings, clothing, and general life-style of the Quakers. The original meeting house was built at this time.

The first meeting house, however, was considered too small by 1698, for half the population of the town was now Quaker, and Newport had become the site for the annual spring meeting, to which several hundred brethren would travel from Maine, Philadelphia, and the surrounding countryside to meet one another and discuss political and religious issues.

Early settler Nicholas Easton's wife left the plot of land on which the Great Meeting House was constructed, and work began on this medieval-style structure, made of wood, in 1699. The interior was furnished with simple benches for seating and, apart from this austere furniture, the building, redolent of a barn, was bare of all decoration. In 1729 a North Meeting was added: a two-story extension, the upper story of which was referred to as the "Ship Room," as it was built like a ship's cabin.

Restoration of the Meeting House began in 1967. It was a complicated task, as the building had been extended at least five times (in 1705, 1729, 1807, 1858, and 1867). The architect responsible for the restoration project, Orin M. Bullock, decided that the work should aim to re-create the building as it would have appeared between 1807 and 1858, so that some of the original structure was visible but its evolution was not entirely hidden.

Above: *These massive crossed timbers once braced the original building's turret.*

Opposite: *The severe benches and galleries at one time accommodated more than five hundred members of the Society of Friends.*

Trinity Church, 1725

But the steeple stands foremost in our thoughts, as well as locally. It impresses us as a giant, with a mind comprehensive and discriminating enough to care for the great and small concerns of all the town.
Twice-Told Tales, *Nathaniel Hawthorne*

Opposite: *Trinity Church's gleaming steeple is the focal point of the oldest Episcopal parish in New England.*

Trinity Church is the most delicate building in Newport. Its white, tiered steeple reaches up into the clouds like a frosted stalagmite—the focal point on entry to the harbor.

Richard Munday built the church in 1725, basing his design on the work of Sir Christopher Wren. It is recorded that this church bears a remarkable similarity to Wren's St. Catherine's of Blackfriars, which was razed in the Great Fire of London (1666). It is, however, a more immediate replica of Christ Church, Boston. As a colonial structure, it was built in wood rather than stone, adding to its frail charm. Though the spire was designed in 1726, it was not constructed until 1741 and then, following a gale in 1768, was dismantled and re-erected.

Though the profession of architect was not recognized in the mid-eighteenth century, it is clear from a document that Munday was paid twenty-five pounds for "draughting a plan" for the church. Though he called himself a house carpenter and innkeeper, he can be referred to as Newport's first professional architect.

Money was raised to establish the church through subscriptions. Each member or family of the parish could pay for a certain square footage of the church floor to cordon off as a box pew. For this reason, the box pews are of varied dimensions throughout the sanctuary. Inevitably, during the Gilded Age, the rich socialites left their mark on the church by customizing their pews with the upholstery of their family livery or installing new pieces of furniture for their added comfort.

The focal point of the church is the magnificent triple-tiered wineglass pulpit, the only one in the United States, which faces an organ imported from Robert Bridges of London and donated by Bishop Berkeley.

The church welcomed many important characters in Newport's history besides Berkeley, whose daughter is buried in the graveyard. George Washington is known to have attended a service here in 1781. Admiral de Ternay, the commander of the French fleet during the Revolutionary War, and Chevalier de Fayelle, aide-de-camp to Lafayette, are buried in the shadow of the clapboard church.

Above: *Molding profiles of the round-headed window frames cast a striking shadow across Trinity's clapboards.*

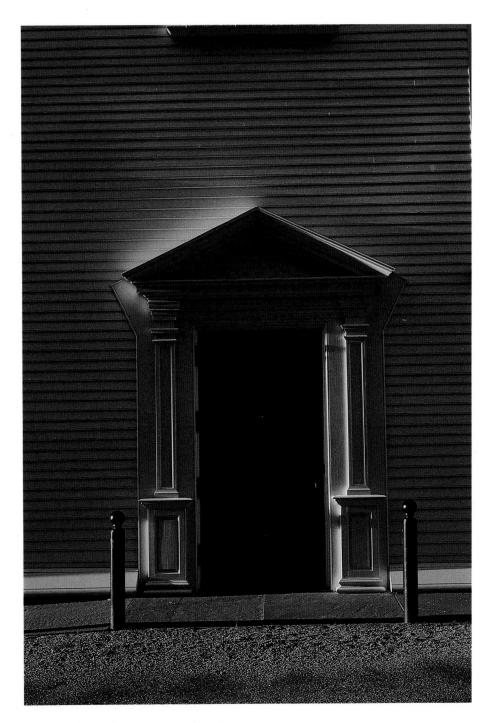

Above: *The south entry is a product of the craftsman's inventiveness: Slender pilasters carry the molded pediment.*

The Redwood Library, 1748

Opposite: *A replica statue of Washington by Houdin stands in front of the library.*

£500 sterling for the purchasing of a library of all arts and sciences, whereunto the curious and impatient enquirer, after resolution of doubts, and the bewildered ignorant might freely repair for the discovery and demonstration of the one, and time, knowledge and satisfaction of the other.

the first directors of the Redwood Library, in recognition of their founder, Abraham Redwood's, wishes

Abraham Redwood's chief concern was that his bequest should be spent on books, rather than on the building itself. He had a captive and hungry audience: At the beginning of the eighteenth century, several wealthy men and women of various religious persuasions were keen to acquire academic knowledge during this age of enlightenment in such a freethinking town. Furthermore, Redwood had a very personal reason for establishing a library: He had been continually frustrated in his efforts to find books for his children's education.

The erection of the library, the seventh in America, was the outcome of the local Philosophical Club, which had been founded in 1730 and whose original members included Peter Bours, Bishop Berkeley, Henry Collins, Abraham Redwood, and twenty-five others. Collins donated the land, formerly known as the "Bowling Greene," and Peter Harrison, a young English architect, was selected to design the building. Harrison had worked with Vanbrugh on Blenheim Palace in England, the home of the Duke of Marlborough.

A total of £5,000 was raised from subscriptions, and building commenced. It was Harrison's first commission in Newport and a handsome tribute to his talent. He designed a wooden version of a Roman Doric temple, taking his inspiration from the headpiece of Book IV of Edward Hoppus's *Palladio,* which showed Kent's façade for Lord Burlington's garden temples at Chiswick. The decorative details were lifted from Battey Langley's 1745 *Theory of Design.* Harrison conceived the design in London and is known to have owned both of these books.

What is remarkable about this building, apart from its academic purity, is the fact that it is not only the first classical building in America, predating its successors by decades, but that there were very few of this style found even in Europe at the time.

The ordered proportion and noble, understated decoration render it a calm and inspiring building in which to study. Like most New England structures of the day, the library was built of wood, which was then rusticated and painted to imitate stone. Major extensions have been added without spoiling its lines: George

Snell's reading room in 1858, George C. Mason's delivery room in 1875, Gardner B. Perry's stacks in 1913, and Irving B. Haynes's stacks in 1987.

Such concern for public education was not without precedent in the Redwood family. It is recorded that Abraham's great-great uncle donated a building for the founding of the Bristol Library in England, one of the first free libraries. The bulk of the books, which reflected Abraham Redwood's (and his friends') interest in the humanities, history, geography, and the classics, were purchased from England and the Continent for the Library. There was only one work of fiction, Fielding's *Joseph Andrews.* This was not surprising, however, given that the novel, as a literary mode, was still in its infancy.

Opposite: *The octagonal Summer House once stood on the grounds of Redwood's Portsmouth estate.*

Above: *Harrison's "Venetian" windows were originally located on the rear elevation of the library.*

The Touro Synagogue, 1763

Opposite: *The synagogue was built at an angle to the street so that the Ark of the Covenant would face Jerusalem.*

How came they here? What burst of Christian hate;
What persecution merciless and blind,
Drove o'er the sea,—that desert, desolate—
These Ishmaels and Hagars of mankind?
The Jewish Cemetery at Newport, *Henry Wadsworth Longfellow*

The Jews arrived in Newport in 1656 from Europe and the West Indies. They were drawn by the town charter, secured by Dr. John Clarke, which guaranteed "liberty of conscience." For a hundred years they worshipped in their own homes until Isaac de Touro, a wealthy businessman originally from Amsterdam, left $10,000 of his estate to build a synagogue.

This is the oldest synagogue in America and is a lasting tribute to Newport's religious tolerance. The third building in town designed by Peter Harrison, the synagogue was begun in 1759 and completed in 1763.

The synagogue is severe, elegant, and classical. As an Englishman, Harrison was familiar with the work of Kent and Inigo Jones, and as he had no precedent upon which to base his synagogue design, he used motifs seen on earlier Sephardic synagogues in London and Amsterdam, and the Palladian model shown in Kent's book, *Designs of Inigo Jones and Others*. The details owe their inspiration to plates found in Battey Langley's book, *Theory of Design*.

Harrison ensured that the building incorporated the traditional twelve columns, representing the twelve tribes of Israel. The focal point of the interior is the Ark of the Covenant, required by custom to be placed on a wall facing Jerusalem (hence the building's placement at a diagonal to the street). The hall of worship is divided into two stories, the upper supported by the twelve columns, capped with two classical orders; Ionic on the lower floor and Corinthian on the upper. Traditionally, the women would enter by the back staircase and sit upstairs, the men below, for the separation of the sexes was supposed to ensure concentration during worship.

During the American Revolution, the British, while stripping the entire town for firewood and destroying nearly 500 houses, honored the sanctity of the synagogue and left it standing. Consequently, in 1780 it was used as the meeting place for the General Assembly of Rhode Island, as it was one of the few surviving buildings.

Above: *The twelve Ionic columns that support the gallery represent the twelve tribes of Israel.*

Opposite: *The "Pulpit for Reading Law" is located at the center of the synagogue.*

Nichols-Wanton-Hunter House, 1748

Opposite: *Nichols had his mansion constructed in English fashion, with clapboards over brick-filled walls.*

Slaves, rum and molasses; a dark brown trade,
The brown skins shining
With the gleam of sweat, The brown drink gleaming
Through the upraised glass;
The thick brown syrup, kegged and rolled,
Swaying with the rhythm of the wave-slopped hold.
Triangular Trade, *Frances Minturn Howard*

Built on Easton's Point, overlooking the harbor, this handsome clapboard house was home to two prominent Newport merchants, Jonathan Nichols, Jr., and Colonel Joseph Wanton, Jr. Its vantage point over the water enabled these men to watch their ships sailing back and forth, laden with the spoils of triangular trade: molasses, rum, and slaves.

Originally, the house faced seaward and was only half its current width when built by Nichols. He not only accumulated great wealth but also earned a political position in the nascent community, becoming colonial deputy and then deputy governor in 1753. After his death, three years later, his brother sold the house and adjoining property to Wanton, who was descended from a Massachusetts Quaker family. Like the previous owner, Wanton involved himself in local politics and was elected to the Assembly in 1756, at the age of twenty-six.

However, Wanton was a Tory, loyal to the British throne and supportive of the unpopular Stamp Act, which had been imposed on the colonies. In attempting to defend Newport from the revolutionaries, he was captured by the American troops and then forced to flee Newport when the French occupied the town.

The house then rose to fulfill a very significant political role: It became the headquarters and residence of the commander of the French fleet, Admiral de Ternay. Sadly, the house witnessed the death of this great leader but continued to serve its revolutionary purpose as the headquarters for the French officers while they successfully defeated the British fleet, freeing the colony.

A deep depression followed the Revolutionary War and the house, like the surrounding buildings, suffered. It fell into disrepair until it was bought by William Hunter in 1805. Hunter, the son of a distinguished Scottish physician who was the first to lecture on anatomy in America, was a lawyer. Again, politics preoccupied the household, for Hunter was elected to the General Assembly in 1799 and later became a senator. His family remained in the house until 1863, though most of the servants did not stay long, driven away by Hunter's notoriously harsh discipline.

Opposite: *The broken pediment above the doorway embraces a carved wooden pineapple, a symbol of hospitality.*

Above: *The main entrance hall has raised panel wainscoting and a dividing elliptical arch set on scroll brackets.*

Opposite: *The northwest room is dominated by a large working fireplace with a built-in beehive oven.*

Above: *Wanton had the carved pine Corinthian pilasters painted to imitate black marble veined with gold.*

Above: *Mahogany from Santo Domingo was used to carve the main staircase.*

Opposite: *The dining room's rich floor-to-ceiling bolection paneling is "spreckled" in a pattern simulating walnut.*

Whitehall, 1729

The inhabitants are of a mixed kind, consisting of many sects and subdivisions of sects. Here are four sorts of Anabaptists, besides Presbyterians, Quakers, and independents, and many of no profession at all. Notwithstanding so many differences, there are fewer quarrels about religion that elsewhere, the people living peaceably with their neighbours of whatever persuasion.

from a letter by Bishop Berkeley, 1729

Opposite: *Whitehall was built "in loyal remembrance of the palace of the English kings from Henry VIII to James II."*

The "Irish Plato," Bishop Berkeley, a follower of the Church of England, was a confirmed advocate of religious tolerance. He had mixed with the literary and philosophical coterie in London, where he had been introduced to the court by Jonathan Swift. In 1729 Berkeley had set sail for America en route to Bermuda, where he intended to found a Church of England school to bring Christianity to the Indians. He was unaware that there were no Indians in Bermuda at the time! His intention was to await the £20,000 grant promised by the British government and then continue on the last leg of his journey.

Despite the fact that he was in transit, the three years he spent on Rhode Island were to prove very fruitful both for the Bishop and for the citizens of Newport. He not only wrote his well-received philosophical tract, entitled *Alciphron; or The Minute Philosopher,* which was based on Platonic dialogues, but also helped found the Newport Literary and Philosophical Society in 1730, through which the Redwood Library came into existence. Berkeley purchased the ninety-six acres of farmland, on which he built his temporary home, from Joseph and Sarah Whipple for £2,500. Whitehall, named in tribute to the British royal palace of that name, was a simple abode—a large wooden farmhouse designed with the help of his friend, the English architect Sir John James. Standing alone in a beautiful valley, it was just half a mile from Second Beach. The restrained simplicity of the dwelling was enobled by a fine, wide doorway surmounted by a low pediment supported by Ionic pilasters.

Whitehall became a center for the intelligentsia of Newport, who would travel the three miles to visit the Berkeley family in their idyllic rural setting. The family worshipped at Trinity Church and were greatly loved for their tolerance of religious dissent and for their encouragement of discussion and learning. Before leaving Newport, where he was so happy, Berkeley donated an English organ to the church, his library to Yale, and founded a scholarship at the university named after his home. He eventually returned to England, for the promised grant never arrived.

Above: *At the entrance, Berkeley added a blind left door panel to maintain genuine Palladian proportions.*

Opposite: *The broad-shingled roof of the rear lean-to, or saltbox, extends northward behind the symmetrical façade.*

Vernon House, 1760

In no instance has nature made the satellite larger than its primary planet; and as England and America, with respect to each other, reverse the common order of nature, it is evident that they belong to different systems. England to Europe: America to itself.
Common Sense, *Thomas Paine*

Opposite: *Vernon House is one of Newport's finest high-style Georgian mansions.*

Vernon House, a handsome colonial or English Georgian-style building, took its name from its second owner, William Vernon. It was built for Metcalf Bowler, a trader, and it is possible that Peter Harrison was the architect. Bowler was a staunch advocate of independence and was the first to hold a lavish celebratory dinner when the bitterly criticized Stamp Act was repealed. William Vernon bought the house in 1773, on the eve of the Revolutionary War. He fled the advance of the British, burying the family silver and suffering the British occupancy of his home. Vernon, a man of letters, was a committed supporter of freedom and independence. "If we establish our rights and liberty upon a firm and lasting basis," he wrote, "on the winding up of this bloody contest, I am content." He devoted his labors to the Council and, as president of the Eastern Navy Board, based in Boston, he was instrumental in founding the American Navy. With the arrival of the French fleet, Vernon lent his home to the commander of the French forces, Count de Rochambeau, and it became navy headquarters. Here, Rochambeau and George Washington drew up their campaigns.

While in residency, Rochambeau instructed that an extension be built on the north side, called the "French Hall," where councils of war were held and where, by night, the French officers entertained their gracious Newport hosts. Many a Franco-American romance blossomed as the guests danced the quadrille, a form of square dance introduced at the French court in 1773. Another Franco-American *affair d'amour* was being conducted by William Vernon's son, who had been sent to France to be educated under the guidance of a family friend, Benjamin Franklin. The young Vernon befriended the doomed Marie Antoinette and returned to Newport with an extraordinary gift from her: one of the three known (though disputed) versions of Leonardo da Vinci's *Mona Lisa*—entitled *The Nun* at the time. On returning to his home town, Vernon was dubbed "Count Vernon" as he cut a dashing figure, flaunting his Continental manners and flamboyant French style of dress.

Above: *In the northwest parlor, wall paintings in the Chinese style were discovered in 1937 behind paneling.*

Above: *Chinese-style wall paintings were applied directly over the smooth plaster walls to simulate lacquered wood panels.*

Prescott Farm, Early 1700s

Our rural vernacular developed in ignorance, not in knowledge; instinctively, not self-consciously; it was wrought by the hands of artisans, and not of an educated architectural profession.
The Century Magazine, *1886*

Opposite: *The red gambrel-roofed Guard House once stood next to the circa 1730 Prescott House (at left, behind tree).*

This idyllic, early-eighteenth-century country seat of Mr. Henry Overing, a wealthy farmer, was requisitioned in 1777 by General William Prescott, the commander of the British troops on Rhode Island, as his summer headquarters. It is believed that he chose the residence because he was intimate with the lady of the house. Prescott was hated for his brutish, high-handed ways. He became a focus of resentment for the local patriots, and the farm is remembered as the site of a daring feat by the young Major William Barton who decided to avenge the capture of the American General Lee by taking General Prescott. He patiently waited for the right moment, and armed with detailed information about the British headquarters from a British prisoner, he persuaded some of his fellow men, against orders, to attempt this seemingly impossible task. By night, forty men sailed in whale boats to the shore a mile from Prescott farm, stormed the house against all odds, and took the general, still in his nightshirt, and two others. Prescott was imprisoned in Providence and then exchanged for General Lee.

The estate eventually passed into the hands of Bradford Norman, a wealthy businessman who owned the property across the street, and then to his daughter, Mrs. Cook. In 1970 the Newport Restoration Foundation bought and restored the farm and re-erected the picturesque mill that stands on the grounds. This mill was constructed in 1812 at Warren, Rhode Island, was moved several times, and was badly damaged in a 1938 hurricane before finding its final home at Prescott.

Prescott Farm offers the visitor an evocative and beautifully restored example of an early colonial farmstead. A few miles from Newport proper, it is surrounded by fertile pasture, and its buildings are filled with typical artifacts and furniture of the day, collected from sources throughout Rhode Island.

Above: *The Guard House's eight-over-twelve-paned, double-hung window is typical of early Georgian detailing.*

Opposite: *The Old Grist Mill, built in Warren, Rhode Island, in 1812, was moved to and restored at Prescott Farm.*

Elmhyrst, 1835

Consider the momentous event in architecture when the wall parted and the column became.
Louis I. Kahn

Opposite: *The entry façade at Elmhyrst is composed around four monumental Ionic columns.*

Russell Warren's handsome house was built in 1835 for William Vernon, and is considered to be one of the finest examples of the Greek revival style in America. Warren was a British architect who designed many of his buildings for American clients. Vernon was a member of the famous mercantile family of Newport who had built Vernon House (p. 54) before the Revolution. It is based on a square plan without the portico and pediment associated with a temple, and according to architectural historians Antoinette Downing and Vincent Scully, it was constructed by Talman and Bucklin of Providence.

The attic story was removed, which renders the house somewhat unbalanced. Warren maintained the Greek theme with the addition of an office and porter's lodge, built in imitation of single-story Greek temples. Downing and Scully regret that "the (landscaped) estate has been broken up and all this is now lost, but Elmhyrst in the past, distinguished as it was by broad simplicity of form, warmth of detail, and finely conceived proportions, was one of Newport's great architectural achievements."

The Greek revival in America began in the 1820s. The ancient Greek ideals of democracy and the contemporary struggle of the Greeks to gain independence from their Ottoman oppressors understandably inspired sympathy from a nation that had so recently won its own freedom from the British colonists. Elmhyrst is a noble and refined architectural expression of the triumph of these ideals.

Above: *The full gable front and encircling colonnade of the annex are reminiscent of a Greek temple.*

Opposite: *The front doorway of the annex is surrounded by an overhead transom window and flanking sidelights.*

Kingscote, 1841

The doors and windows of the large square house were all wide open, to admit the purifying sunshine, which lay in generous patches upon the floor of a wide, high, covered piazza adjusted to two sides of the mansion—a piazza on which several straw-bottomed rocking-chairs and half a dozen of those small cylindrical stools in green and blue porcelain, which suggest an affiliation between the residents and the Eastern trade, were symmetrically disposed.
The Europeans, *Henry James*

Opposite: *Kingscote's asymmetrical massing picturesquely relates the demurely scaled villa to its site.*

"I recollect a plan of a cottage—two stories in front—which you showed me some time ago, which with a few alterations I think will suit my views," George Noble Jones informed his architect Richard Upjohn in 1839. This was to be the first "summer cottage" built along the now-prestigious Bellevue Avenue, then a rough dirt road, and it provided a model for many subsequent wooden "cottages" built in the fashionable Gothic style. The Gothic touch is evident in the drip molds over the windows and the bargeboard under the eaves. It is a very early example of the cottage *ornée,* as it is picturesque rather than monumental, and in perfect harmony with the surrounding treescape.

The site and the relation of the building to the surrounding landscape were symptomatic of the mid-nineteenth-century desire of the educated to turn their backs on the ugliness of industrial progress and re-embrace the beauty of nature.

Vincent Scully, the architectural historian, noted that, "It represents the romantic yearning toward nature which has since been derided as a corrupt sentimentality but which, in a deeper sense, is rather part of that search for freer systems and more natural values which characterized some of the most creative aspects of nineteenth-century thought."

Though the house was large, by contemporary standards, Upjohn successfully broke up its mass, using numerous gables and designing the structure on largely asymmetrical lines, ridding it of any rigid formality.

The house was originally painted a gentle buff color, and the paint was mixed with sand to give the impression of masonry. The gray-and-maroon paintwork now apparent on the building was not applied until the next owner, William Henry King, bought it in 1864 and recolored it. During the Civil War, the Jones family moved back to Savannah, Georgia, and John R.A. Griswold rented the house while he was having his home, Griswold House (p. 80), built.

The Kings were an old Newport family; an ancestor had been one of the first doctors in town and was credited with introducing the smallpox vaccine to the area. By the nineteenth century, the family business was centered on the China trade, with offices in Canton. Having amassed a fortune in the East, William King returned to Newport, bought this house, which he renamed Kingscote, or King's Cottage, and installed his Eastern treasures, including paintings by the Irishman George Chinnery and his Chinese pupils. Over the fireplace in the library hangs a portrait of the famous Mandarin trader, Houqua, given to King by the sitter.

In 1875 Kingscote was passed on to William's nephew, David, who decided to redecorate, initially employing George Champlin Mason and then, in 1878, Stanford White.

Before the Civil War, there was no real "season" for those who owned summer cottages in Newport, and a very informal life-style was favored. Formal dinners were certainly not fashionable, except among men. One of the reasons that David King wanted a new dining-room extension was that formal dining had become de rigueur in the 1880s, with dinners sometimes lasting as long as three hours—a custom that one wit referred to as the "battle of the dining hours."

White's mandate was to construct a larger dining room over which he was to build additional bedrooms and a nursery. Though only twenty-five, he handled the commission magnificently, by introducing the bold sensibilities of the Aesthetic movement to the project. Developing the original organic theme, White concentrated on the Queen Anne style, using shingles, clapboards, and large expanses of glass. The entrance to the dining room is a mahogany screen of colonial and Moorish inspiration, while the windows set on either side of the fireplace are inset with blue and green colored glass, known as Tiffany brick, which turns a brilliant copper color in the afternoon sun. These colored panes hid the service quarters from view. Like Upjohn, whose signature was the curved wall, White also left his trademark, the dahlia flower, which appears throughout the house.

Opposite: *Layered wall planes set off Gothic details: battlements, pointed arch windows, and decorative bargeboards.*

Above: *The entry dormer has projecting curvilinear bargeboards embracing an engaged finial.*

Above: *In 1878 Stanford White added three stories to the west side of the cottage, including an elaborate dining room.*

Opposite: *In deference to Upjohn's details, White added diamond-pane windows set within corner-gabled dormers.*

Opposite: *Entrance to the dining room is gained through the gates of a removable spool-and-spindle mahogany screen.*

Above: *The parquet floor and wainscoting extend beyond the screen to bring the dining room out into the hallway.*

Above: *The spacious Queen Anne-inspired dining room was built large enough to double as a ballroom.*

Opposite: *The dining-room is dominated by a yellow Siena marble fireplace flanked by Tiffany-glass bricks.*

Malbone Hall, 1848-49

Opposite: *Malbone Hall recalls the castellated ruins of eighteenth-century English garden architecture.*

There was Manderley, our Manderley, secretive and silent as it had always been, the grey stone shining in the moonlight of my dream, the mullioned windows reflecting the green lawns and the terrace. Time could not wreck the perfect symmetry of those walls, nor the site itself, a jewel in the hollow of a hand.
Rebecca, *Daphne du Maurier*

Like Manderley, the original Malbone Hall was razed by fire in 1766. It had been the magnificent country estate of Colonel Godfrey Malbone, a blunderbusting slave-trade merchant from Virginia, who had commissioned Richard Munday to build him a pink sandstone mansion to proclaim his trading success. Mischievously mindful to avoid customs duties, he had an underground tunnel constructed down to the sea, along which he received contraband goods.

Malbone became a great social center—even its fiery end was witnessed by a group of guests. During a large dinner party, the kitchen chimney caught fire, and the flames spread rapidly through the house. Before the firemen could contain the blaze, Malbone had burnt down. Colonel Malbone was unfazed: He ordered that dinner be served in an adjacent building, cavalierly explaining that, "If I have lost my house, that is no reason why we should lose our dinners."

For a century, the ivy-covered ruin lay in its overgrown parkland until the New York lawyer, Jonathan Prescott Hall, decided to commission Alexander Jackson Davis to build him a new home. The Gothic masterpiece, calling to mind the castellated ruins that have been immortalized in such English novels as Jane Austen's *Northanger Abbey,* was, like the original, built in pink sandstone. Hall took particular trouble to restore the grounds, which had been Malbone's pride. Mrs. Martha J. Lamb wrote in *The Homes of America* (1879) that "he restocked the ruined grounds with marble fauns, naiads, hamadryads, and nymphs, after the taste of the olden period." Hall was an expert in botany and particularly ornithology. An extension to the library was eventually added to the house, just to contain his ornithological books and his collection of stuffed birds.

Malbone Hall was one of the pioneer "summer cottages" in Newport. As it is set away from the town center and located on the opposite side of town from the Bellevue Avenue and Ocean Drive district, it has maintained its tranquil seclusion and stands on a reasonable plot of ground, unlike the "white elephants" along the Cliff Walk.

Above: *Malbone Hall's side elevation is anchored at the corner by the staircase turret with battlements.*

Opposite: *The varied roof line and multiple gables were key elements in the Gothic revival's romantic language.*

Griswold House, 1861-63

The air of those rooms was saturated with a fine bouquet of silence so nourishing, so succulent, that I never went into them without a sort of greedy anticipation.
Remembrance of Things Past, *Marcel Proust*

The Griswold House, commissioned by John Noble Alsop Griswold, was Richard Morris Hunt's first building in Newport. He returned from the Ecole de Beaux Arts in Paris, where he had been the first American student, and though he was trained in the grand style of European architecture, at the time he did not feel that this style was appropriate for the American environment or way of life. Consequently, he designed a series of wood-framed buildings that are considered to be the best of his work and that were later christened by the architectural historian Vincent Scully as the "Stick Style." Hunt preferred these buildings to the grand, ornate palazzi he designed later.

Griswold House was built between 1861 and 1863, in what was called, at the time, the "modern Gothic style." The house was inspired by European rustic architecture; it was a synthesis of the *pavillions d'amour* in the Bois de Boulogne in Paris and the half-timbered medieval structures that had prevailed throughout northern and central Europe for many centuries.

A very prominent site was acquired on Bellevue Avenue, adjoining the Redwood Library, and in contrast to the formal and classical lines of its neighbor, Hunt chose an asymmetrical, picturesque composition broken up by a multitude of gables, bay windows, and porches. The bones of the building were (in theory) exposed with the use of timber posts, beams, and diagonal braces, creating a homey informal look.

Sarah Bradford Landau, in her study of the Continental Picturesque, described the typical Stick Style dwelling as "a wood house of irregular and picturesque outlines, projecting and bracket-supported form, and balconies, big, woody gables, wraparound verandas and clapboard walls articulated by horizontal, vertical and diagonally placed boards." The Griswold house was an early and important precedent of this form. Landau revealed that, though the half-timbering was exposed to suggest the actual framework, in fact it was a purely decorative effect, bearing no relationship to the building's actual skeleton.

The renaissance of this vernacular, timbered picturesque style came about in France, Germany, and America as the successful middle classes began to commission holiday homes in resort areas. Griswold had made his fortune in the China trade. While the Griswolds were living in Paris, Hunt was a house guest and was commissioned to design their Newport summer residence.

The interior of the building is as complicated as the exterior. Hunt designed a honeycomb layout for the major rooms, each interlocked at various angles to the central hall. This invited a flow of people from one room to another and also enhanced the circulation of air. The Art Association now owns the building, which was remodeled for them in 1916, and regularly exhibits both local historic collections and contemporary artworks.

Samuel Pratt House, 1871-72

Opposite: The rustic perforated gambrel gable and polychromed slate siding are typical features of Hunt's early work.

When they came quite up to the little house they saw that it was built of bread and covered with cakes, but that the windows were of clear sugar. "We will set to work on that," said Hansel, "and have a good meal"
Hansel and Gretel, *the Brothers Grimm*

Samuel Pratt was a man of leisure for most of his life. Though he is known to have been an architect, his primary income was derived from the royalties of a patented improvement to the sewing machine. His Bellevue Avenue house, also known as "Bird's Nest Cottage," is probably the work of Richard Morris Hunt and is an extreme example of the picturesque Chalet style that emerged in the United States in the period after the Civil War. It may also have been designed by Pratt himself, as it is recorded in the Hazard Ford & Company 1872 Newport real estate circular. The house is tiny and coyly charming. Architectural historian Vincent Scully aptly referred to the house as *mignon.* A number of minute and decorative towers crown the residence. Swiss-style carvings decorate the roof. The house is a fairy-tale fantasy, a cozy little gingerbread structure.
Pratt, who was from Boston, used the house as a summer home until about 1917. It has since been restored and converted into a real estate office.

Watts Sherman House, 1875

My precept to all who build is that the owner should be an ornament to the house, and not the house to the owner.
Cicero

Opposite: *Richardson's design of the Watts Sherman house introduced the Queen Anne style to America.*

William Watts Sherman, a physician by training and a banker by profession, is fondly remembered as a philanthropist and a scholar, and was described by Maud Elliot, a local writer, as a "living encyclopaedia of Newportiana." He was given the land on which to build his summer house by his father-in-law and immediate neighbor, George Peabody Wetmore of Château-sur-Mer. Watts Sherman commissioned Henry Hobson Richardson (the second American to study at the Ecole de Beaux Arts in Paris) to design the house, which was acknowledged as one of the most important examples of American architecture in the 1870s. The young architect Stanford White was working in Richardson's offices at the time, and consequently, it is debatable how much of the design input was White's and how much was Richardson's.
The house was based on the old English manor style which had been popularized by Richard Norman Shaw in Surrey, southeast England. It is generally referred to as American Queen Anne style, a precursor of the Shingle Style, being picturesque yet simple in form. The free use of shingles cut in various forms, which have weathered in the sea breezes to a delicate silvery-gray, the half-timbering, and the painted patterns on the stucco panels give the house its decorative distinction. The ground-floor story of the house is constructed in red-and-gray granite, the upper story features shingles, and the roof is impaled by handsome, high, red-brick chimneys.
Between 1879 and 1881 the interiors, following Richardson's recommendation, were designed by Stanford White. The house is centered around a large living hall paneled in dark, rich mahogany, like the skin of a freshly-fallen horse chestnut, which is dominated by an imposing mahogany staircase. All the reception rooms lead off this area, including White's magnificent library, which was added in 1880. The library is an amalgamation of the American colonial style that was returning to fashionable favor and the chinoiserie of Chippendale. In simulation of Oriental lacquer work, the room is lined with shelves, drawers, and secret compartments lacquered in green and gold.
Richardson, like Richard Morris Hunt, is acclaimed as one of the great American architects of the nineteenth century and is credited with helping to bring a sense of identity to American architecture, which was suffering from mediocrity and confusion in the 1850s and 1860s. At the time, Calvert Vaux, one of the architects of Central Park, wrote, "A sense of starvation is beginning to be felt, and wherever a small supply of food arrives it seems to be accepted gratefully if there is any flavor in it." Richardson's Romanesque and Shingle-style designs were to provide such sweetmeats.
The Watts Sherman house is now a dormitory for the students of Salve Regina College.

Above: *A Queen Anne sunflower is carved into the bargeboards and posts of the recessed porch.*

Above: *The monumental staircase rises above the living hall. Heavy chamfered posts support the staircase and ceiling.*

Baldwin House, 1877-78

I do not know how it was—but, with the first glimpse of the building, a sense of insufferable gloom pervaded my spirit.
The Fall of the House of Usher, *Edgar Allan Poe*

This brooding house gives a ghostly impression, a result, perhaps, of the fast-encroaching woods, which deny light, and the overhanging gables, which throw long, dark shadows across its vistas. Though it was designed as a summer house, it is hard to imagine that uplifting rays have ever penetrated into its gloom. Among the fallen leaves on the lawn, life seems extinguished, perhaps a portent to those who seek entry.
Baldwin House was built in the Queen Anne style on Bellevue Avenue by the New Jersey architects Potter and Robertson for C. H. Baldwin. It later became known as the Prescott Lawrence House. Brick and shingles ascend from the ground up, shadowed by variously timbered gables, and the whole is definitively impaled by a huge vertical chimney mass.

Above: *Below the shingled wall is a half-timbered gable. Dentil molding at the eaves connects the disparate surface planes.*

Opposite: *The ribbed chimney stack rises up the exterior wall to penetrate the extended mass of the third-story gable end.*

The Casino, 1879–81

I first strolled through the entrance and surveyed the playing area and the arrangements for the spectators. The building was designed—as were other edifices in Newport—by the brilliant and ill-fated Stanford White. As in every work from his hand it was marked by a distinguished design and free play of fancy.
Theophilus North, *Thornton Wilder*

Opposite: *Bilateral symmetry unifies the Bellevue Avenue elevation of the Newport Casino, a Shingle Style masterpiece.*

Revenge, following a snub, was the impetus for founding The Casino, one of America's first country clubs. James Gordon Bennet, Jr., the heir to the *New York Herald* newspaper fortune, was a wild and fun-seeking young man. As a prank, he had encouraged his English friend, Captain Henry Candy, to ride a horse into the Newport Reading Room, the resort's most exclusive and conservative club. Candy obliged and Bennet was banned. Bennet and Candy are also remembered for having introduced polo to the United States. Bennet had a point to prove with his prank: Sportsmanship and scandalous frivolity, he believed, would attract a greater portion of Newport society than strict rules and stuffiness. He decided to build a club that everyone would want to join.

Bennet bought a prime sight on Bellevue Avenue, opposite his home, and commissioned McKim, Mead & White to draw up plans for a social center, open to both sexes, in this rapidly expanding resort town. It was the firm's first masterpiece in Newport. McKim designed the architectural framework, which was then embellished by White, and provided a block of shops on the street, sporting facilities such as a billiard parlor, bowling alley, court tennis (and later lawn tennis), a model opera house, gentlemen's lodgings, a restaurant, reading rooms, and a covered walk along which Newport society paraded. It was both a private and a public club; the private members were elected as shareholders or subscribers who paid an annual subscription, while the public could pay an entrance fee and enjoy most of the club's facilities for the day. The Casino took its name from the Italian word *casina,* meaning "little house," a structure that would typically have been built in the gardens of a great estate. Entering through a decorative archway behind the commercial façade, the visitor is welcomed into a large, horseshoe-shaped court bound by balustrades and shingled curves that embrace the lawns and meet at the apex, which is marked by a handsome, spherical clock tower. Though the architectural composition of these buildings is classical, the decorative details are eclectic and picturesque, being drawn from American, French, and Japanese motifs. The woodwork and lathe-turned spindle screens, for example, are Japanese in inspiration, perhaps specifically inspired by the Japanese pavilions at the Centennial Exhibition of 1876 in Philadelphia, while the frieze of sunflowers above the second-story windows (which have been removed) were borrowed from the English Aesthetic movement.

The Casino is a spectacular example of a building erected in sympathy with, rather than in contrast to, nature. Its shady, curvaceous walkways, undulating rooftops, and juxtaposed gables, its skin of shingles, like the taut scales of a snake, and its pine-green-painted, carved walkways, which provide dappled shade from the sun-drenched courts, acclaim the architect's alliance with nature.

In 1881 the Casino became the first site of the National Lawn Tennis Tournament, which, beginning in 1915, was hosted by Forest Hills (for reasons of practicality, not least of which was the continuous chattering of the Newport society ladies and lolling bachelors along the balustrades). It was a bitterly fought campaign that became known as "the battle of the stadium against the vari-coloured parasols of Newport."

The Casino is now home to the International Tennis Hall of Fame.

Above: *Over the entrance, the central gable consists of a screened Palladian motif perforating the shingled skin.*

Above: *A secondary gable within a main gable is slightly corbeled outward to show off inset windows and carved ornament.*

Following pages: *The Casino's interior courtyard is embraced at the east end by a crescent-shaped horseshoe piazza.*

Opposite: *The turrets of the châteaux of the Loire were the inspiration for the shingled tower with bell-shaped roof.*

Above: *The combination of variegated, diamond, and plain square-butted shingle patterns promotes a textural richness.*

Above: *Spindlework screening and grilled panels of the railings suggest the influence Japanese architecture had on White.*

Opposite: *From the horseshoe piazza, one has a view of the grass tennis courts and two rear buildings.*

Isaac Bell House, 1882-83

There is religion in everything around us—a calm and holy religion in the unbreathing things of nature, which every man would do well to imitate.

John Ruskin

Compared to its overdressed neighbors, the understated attire of the Isaac Bell house proclaims its confidence and discretion. The house is well suited to its surroundings, clothed in tawny shingles and decorated with bamboo details. Its luxury is that of simplicity. The house was designed by McKim, Mead & White and is one of the most successful Shingle Style buildings of the period. It embraces its wooded grounds with wide, open porches, supported by imitation bamboo posts. This decorative detail suggests an Oriental influence favored at the end of the nineteenth century. The porches provide open-air settings for their occupants, who could see and be seen from fashionable Bellevue Avenue. Despite its size, it is a very delicate house, and the variegated patterning of the shingles shows a sensitive consideration to small details. Indeed, they seem to change in color like the leaves as the seasons pass. Unlike its cold, marbled neighbors, this house has evolved with time; it is certainly no "white elephant."

The plan of the building fans out from a large central hall, warmed by a massive hearth, and each major reception room enjoys a special vantage point overlooking the grounds. Nature is the focal point throughout; from its very construction materials to its vistas, the role of the house—as a summer residence—is emphasized. The rooms do not relate symmetrically to one another but are interwoven, creating a collage of spaces as one moves through the building. Architect/critic Arnold Lewis considered it to be a "bold artistic venture. The designers rejected the safe road—order, dignity, proven solutions—in favour of spacial excitement, contrasts (texture and void), variations (multiple shingle patterns), asymmetry of perimeter and skyline, and mixed materials (brick below and shingle above)," (*American Country Houses of the Gilded Age*).

Isaac Bell, Jr., supplemented his inherited income with the profits of cotton trading. In 1877, at the age of thirty-one, he married and retired and commissioned McKim, Mead & White to build the house for $41,000. In later life he was appointed ambassador to the Netherlands by President Grover Cleveland.

Above: *The dark, weathered shingles and irregular roof line integrate the house with its natural surroundings.*

Opposite: *The asymmetrical mass of the upper stories is pierced by encircling piazzas with simulated bamboo posts.*

Hypotenuse, 1870-71

I dare say, love in a cottage is very pleasant; but then it positively must be a cottage orneé: *but would not the same love be a great deal safer in a castle, even if Mammon furnished the fortification?*
Crochet Castle, *Thomas Love Peacock*

Opposite: *Hunt placed a rustic alpine gable over a formal entry portico screened by Doric columns.*

Lying like a crisply starched handkerchief dropped between the trees, this witty summer cottage was built by Richard Morris Hunt for his own use. Hunt purchased a tiny cottage between Hill Top Cottage (his original Newport home) and the corner of Church Street and moved it to a triangle of land at the intersection of Greenough Place and Catherine Street. The "new" house was named for its diagonal positioning at the junction. Hunt gradually redesigned the cottage, joining together disparate sections of early-eighteenth-century structures, and finally icing it with a confection of picturesque chalet-style wooden trimmings, after the German scrollwork that was gaining fashionable appeal. The two-story house is principally symmetrical and is capped with a small attic under the hipped gambrel roof. The entrance is decorated with a Doric-columned portico, over which hangs a rustic, Alpine-style gable.

In 1871 Colonel George E. Waring, Jr., took over the residence, and it is recorded in the family papers that Oscar Wilde, the notorious English writer, visited the family for breakfast while on his 1882 lecture tour of America. Wilde would surely have approved of the decorative facing on the house, a charming addition to the simple structure, for as he pointed out, "The first duty of life is to be as artificial as possible. What the second duty is no one has yet discovered."

In 1901, following Hunt's death, Stanford White added a section to the house, which includes a front and back parlor, the kitchen, and two large bedrooms.

The gingerbread trimmings initially horrified the present owner, Mrs. Thomas, who had intended to remove them. "Now," she says, "I thank God that we ran out of money and didn't do so."

Château-sur-Mer, 1851-52

Opposite: *Château-sur-Mer was the first of the grand Newport mansions to be built of stone.*

One caught a glimpse through the trees of a well-kept lawn and beyond it something like a miniature château, hunting lodge, or pavilion d'amour from times past and gone. More precisely, its original structure was seventeenth century, and the garden and upper story had an eighteenth-century look, and the façades had been restored and somewhat spoilt in the nineteenth century, so that the whole thing had a faintly bizarre character, like that of a superimposed photograph.
The Man Without Qualities, *Robert Musil*

Built in 1852 by Seth Bradford, a local architect, Château-sur-Mer was renovated by Richard Morris Hunt in 1872, thereby utterly changing its appearance from that of a Victorian Gothic house to that of a French baroque castle. Bradford was commissioned by the successful China trade merchant, William Shepard Wetmore, to build a home in Newport that he could live in year-round. It was erected on what was to become the fashionable Bellevue Avenue. As the property extended over forty acres virtually to the sea, it was christened Château-sur-Mer and was the first Newport house to imitate the aristocratic dwellings of the "Old World," a taste that soon spread like wildfire.

William's son, George Peabody Wetmore, inherited the property when he was just sixteen and, upon marriage, he decided to alter the building radically, retaining only the gold salon. Wetmore and his new wife vacated the château and took an extended honeymoon in Europe, lasting nine years. During this time, Richard Morris Hunt set to work enlarging the house.

The height of the building was increased by raising the pitch of the mansard roof, thereby converting the building into a Second Empire-style dwelling. Hunt organized an international collaboration on the interior; Luigi Frullini, the famous Florentine decorator and sculptor, provided the Italian Renaissance-style woodwork in the library and dining room, which was all constructed in his Florentine workshop and shipped to Newport; Gregory and Company, the London cabinetmakers, supplied the Aesthetic-movement furniture and woodwork in the bedrooms; and the Paris firm of Charles Salagnad created the painted panels in imitation of tapestries that decorate the stairwell.

Château-sur-Mer is a dark and gloomy house in the true Victorian tradition, bearing little resemblance to the more typically light-filled Newport summer houses. Hunt believed that every important house should have a great hall, so he created the optical illusion of spaciousness with balconies along the top of the walls, making the forty-foot-high hall appear vast and soaring. Other clever touches include the parquet flooring in the dining room, designed to imitate a herringbone-patterned rug, and a

"tree of life" painted from the entrance, extending up trelliswork to the top story of the house. The griffin appears repeatedly in the carvings, furniture, and even the wallpaper in George's bedroom, which was designed by the Englishman William Burgess—for it was part of the Wetmore family crest.

George's two unmarried daughters subsequently inherited the house and asked their cousin, Ogden Codman, to redecorate the green salon. He chose a Louis XV-style interior and lined the walls in green damask. This provided the perfect backdrop for the family's collection of French decorative arts, which had been amassed on George's extended honeymoon. The room followed the principles laid down by Edith Wharton and Ogden Codman in their famous book *The Decoration of Houses:* "If proportion is the good breeding of architecture. . .symmetry. . .may be defined as the sanity of decoration." Codman's tastes for lightly-painted wooden moldings and French furniture were later popularized by decorator Elsie de Wolfe.

In 1917 architect John Russell Pope was commissioned to close off the entrance facing Bellevue Avenue. He added a bay-windowed alcove and moved the main entrance door to the side of the house, under the porte cochere.

Above: *A reproduction of* The Dying
Gaul *occupies the end niche of the Marble
Hall, originally the main entry foyer.*

Opposite: *The Marble Hall's black and
white tiles were laid during the Hunt
addition of 1872.*

Above: *In 1903 the drawing room became the French Salon, redecorated in the Louis XV style by Ogden Codman.*

Above: *The dining room woodwork was carved in the shop of Florentine designer Luigi Frullini.*

Above: *The main entry is flanked by a gracious oak double staircase. A painted tree of life climbs up the stairwell.*

Opposite: *The morning room is outfitted with white oak Eastlake tables, chairs, and bookcases designed by Hunt.*

Above: *At the center of the library's coffered ceiling is a carved walnut rosette.*

Opposite: *Frullini's Renaissance revival library is fitted with bas-relief carved walnut pilasters and bookcases.*

Ochre Court, 1888-91

The walls of the palace were formed of drifted snow, its doors and windows of the cutting winds. There were more than a hundred rooms in the palace, the largest of them many miles in length. They were all lit up by the Northern Lights, and were all alike, vast, empty, icily cold and dazzlingly white. In the midst of the empty and endless hall of snow lay a frozen lake; it is now broken into a thousand pieces.
The Snow Queen, *Hans Christian Andersen*

The blue Indiana stone of Ochre Court is cold and ungiving; its French late-Gothic-style design gives little consideration to the human dimension. The house is truly one of Henry James's "white elephants." Its eclectic grandeur, an exercise in oneupmanship by Ogden Goelet over his brother Robert, who owned Ochre Point, ousted the more rustic or vernacular Stick and Shingle styles of the 1860s and 1870s. Richard Morris Hunt designed the house, and it is the first example in Newport of a palatial home set not in a parkland, where it belongs, but on a suburban plot.

Size is its very essence; the high roofs, turrets, tall chimneys, and sandstone carvings of gargoyles and griffins reveal its architectural inspiration: Edward VII's palace in Paris. The house is centered on a great arcaded hall that rises three stories, made of Caen stone carved with numerous European symbols of royalty, such as the salamander of François Premier, the fleur de lis, and the porcupine, prized by monarchs for its regal quills. Interspersed among these is a cygnet, lifted from the Goelets' coat of arms. Towering over the hall are twelve life-sized bacchanalian gods, leaning out of the arched ceiling supports.

The interiors combine the decorations and furnishings of imported historic rooms with some fine original craftsmanship. Both the library and the breakfast room were originals imported from France. The hundred-room house was left to Goelet's daughter while she was at Vassar, but she did not want to have it, and in 1947 it became the Salve Regina College.

Above: *Ochre Court's front lawn is simply landscaped with footpaths and terraces down to the Cliff Walk.*

Opposite: *Elliptical-arched Gothic windows on the second floor mimic the openings of the loggia below.*

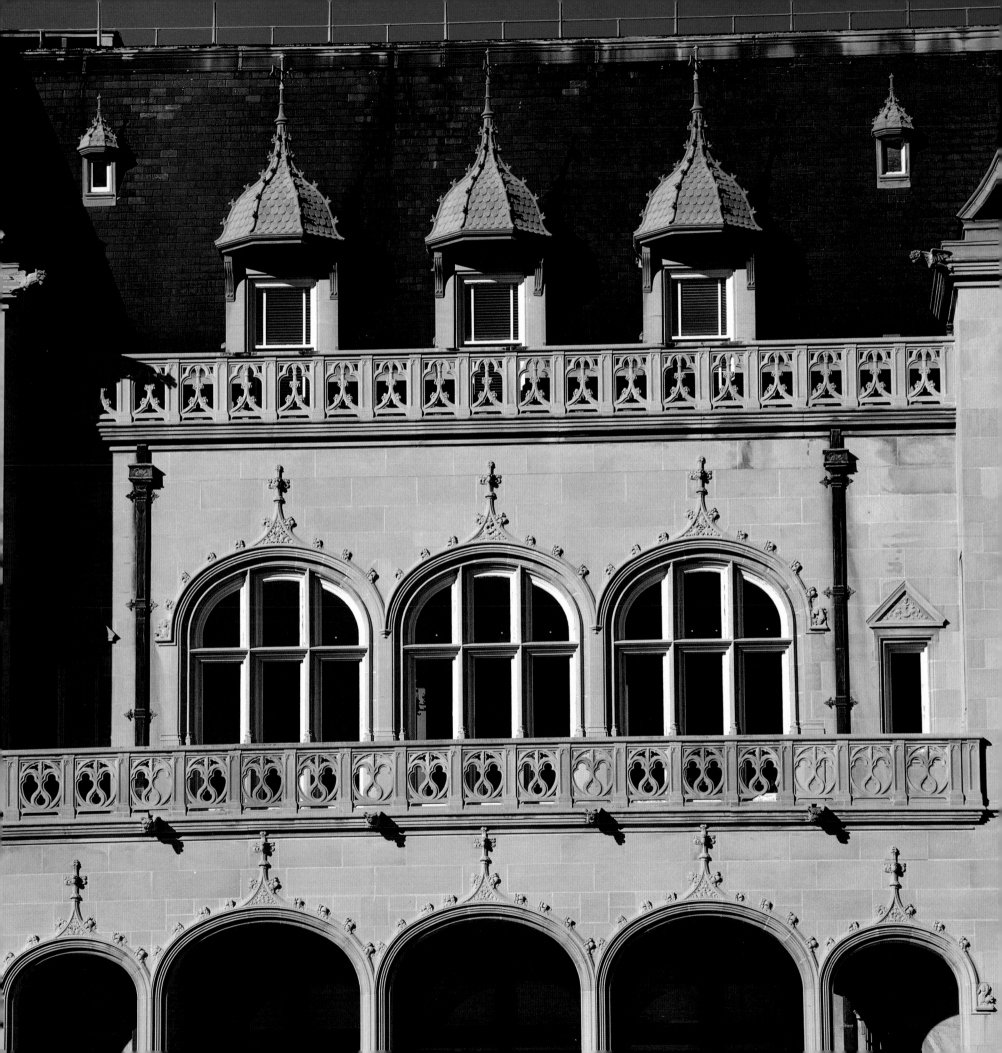

Opposite: *Smooth Indiana limestone wall cladding contrasts with the richly decorated, dormer-filled mansard roof.*

Above: *The south chimney is decorated with a huge carved sundial.*

Above: *Over the entrance, the cornice line of the pavilion is broken by an arched window set below a richly carved dormer.*

Opposite: *Hunt incorporated a variety of sixteenth-century French Renaissance elements in the design of the Château.*

Above: *The staircase, carved from marble and sandstone, has a balustrade supported by dolphins and cupids.*

Opposite: *The interior of Ochre Court is planned around the majestic three-story Gothic-inspired Great Hall.*

Above: *The huge ceiling painting depicts Zeus at the Banquet of the Gods.*

Opposite: *Decorating the Great Hall are gold-leafed figures representing the Liberal and Industrial Arts.*

COMMERCIA   INDUSTRIA

Beacon Rock, 1890-91

Come not to me again: but say to Athens,
Timon hath made his everlasting mansion
Upon the beached verge of the salt flood;
Who once a day with his embossed froth
The turbulent surge shall cover: thither come,
And let my grave-stone be your oracle.
Timon of Athens, *William Shakespeare*

Opposite: *Beacon Rock is situated high above a rocky promontory overlooking Newport Harbor.*

Following spread: *The entrance court was inspired by the peristyle of the Athenian Stoa of Attalos.*

McKim, Mead & White based the designs for Beacon Rock (known as "the Acropolis of Newport") on the ancient Athenian Stoa of Attalos and the adjoining Agora. The mansion was commissioned by Commodore Edwin D. Morgan, the grandson of the governor of New York, as his summer residence.

Erected on a promontory, the house required a remarkable feat of engineering to achieve the impression of being hewn from the very rock of Brenton's Cove. Morgan was determined to build on this spectacular site overlooking the harbor and to overcome the precarious location and ungiving terrain. The rocky, rugged cliffs surround three sides of the house, and the foundations are dug securely into them.

Standing ninety feet above sea level, the front of the house is faced with white marble, while the rest is constructed of stone and brick. In order to transport the building materials onto the site, a magnificent, classical, double-arched causeway was built, which was subsequently disguised by the artful landscaping of Frederick Law Olmsted of New York.

Beacon Rock offers a series of contrasts: the purity of Greek design, of mathematical precision against the rugged, natural setting, promoting a dialogue between civilization and nature. Another contrast is provided by the human-scaled proportions of a house that can be lived in with ease, and the formal façade.

In order to accommodate the changes in terrain dictated by the underlying rock, the house was built on a series of levels, adding memorable character to its interior. Most of the rooms were designed to display European acquisitions, including the octagonal dining room paneled with vintage 1740s mahogany imported from England, an Adams fireplace, and a pair of George III's desks and a matching bureau, reputedly from the Carlton House collection in London.

Morgan was a keen sportsman. He owned successful America's Cup yachts and was president of The New York Yacht Club. His oceangoing steam yacht, *S.Y. Catarina,* was his particular pride. He would sail her around the world with friends, some trips lasting a couple of years.

One idiosyncrasy that Morgan added to the landscape was a wreck, the *Bessie Rogers,* a bark that floundered on Brenton's Cove in 1872. Morgan later salvaged and refloated the picturesque boat, using it both as a gangplank to his own yacht and a mooring for seaside parties.

The other great engineering feat of Beacon Rock is its heating system. Tunnels were blasted out of the rock under the house to receive the sea air, which was sucked inside the tunnels, heated through water, and then pumped into the house above.

This handsome home is now lived in by the celebrated American sculptor Felix de Welden.

Opposite: *The carved marble entry is set behind Ionic columns.*

Above: *The columns carry a marble entablature with a double-banded architrave set below an unadorned frieze.*

Above: *Bisecting a colonnade bay in the entry courtyard of Beacon Rock is one of a pair of Greek statues.*

Opposite: *The materials selected for Beacon Rock help to create a composition that appears to grow out of the landscape.*

Above: *Filigree wrought-iron work arches over the stable's gates, framing a view of Brenton's Cove.*

Above: *The stables at Beacon Rock*
maintain the classical theme.

Above: *The living hall is at the center of an interior plan characterized by a series of free-flowing spaces.*

Opposite: *The oval reception room features scenic wall paintings and an Adamesque plaster ceiling.*

Opposite: *One enters the sunken living room under a cornice with carved dentil blocks and between fluted pilasters.*

Above: *To the west of the living room and overlooking the harbor, the octagonal dining room is reached through an arch.*

Crossways, 1900

O for the doors to be open and an invite with gilded edges
To dine with Lord Lobcock and Count Asthma on platinum benches,
With the somersaults and fireworks, the roast and the smacking
kisses . . .
W. H. Auden

Opposite: *Crossways is an eclectic colonial revival mansion employing basic Palladian design details.*

Eclecticism may have succeeded in the hands of McKim, Mead & White in the 1870s and 1880s, but by the turn of the century, the architects created this "white elephant", a mere cardboard collage of its nobler architectural ancestors. Crossways was built for the Stuyvesant Fish family in 1900.

The house boasts an overscaled colonial portico, which distorts the proportions of the classical building. This glossy and rather brash residence is the home of the parvenu. It sits clumsily on its site, out of harmony with the spectacular surroundings.

Mrs. Stuyvesant Fish commissioned the architects to build her a house after spending several years renting summer "cottages" in Newport. She was a crude but witty woman who ridiculed the strict social etiquette and exclusivity of the resort society. She set herself up as the hostess who provided the most fun for her guests. Though she was neither an aesthete nor an intellectual (indeed, she was unable to spell), she offered amusement to her guests by poking fun at the pomposity of her era.

Mrs. Stuyvesant Fish would serve champagne instead of wine at dinners, in an attempt to "loosen up" what she saw as a rather stuffy group of socialites. She refused to adhere to the local custom of dinner parties that lasted three hours, for she thought them a bore. Her dinners were timed to last fifty minutes.

Despite Mrs. Stuyvesant Fish's eccentric behavior and the fact that she threw parties with more modest budgets than her rival hostesses, an invitation to Crossways was always the most coveted one in town because of the unusual mix of guests and the extraordinary entertainment, which included the vicious wit of the hostess. On being asked by a persistent guest whether she would have one more two-step with him, Mrs. Stuyvesant Fish replied, "Certainly—one upstairs to get your coat, and the other out to your carriage."

Like many competitive hostesses in Newport, Mrs. Stuyvesant Fish generally disliked other women and particularly loathed the tradition of the ladies luncheon. When being dragged along to one such luncheon party, she said upon arrival, "Here you all are, older faces and younger clothes."

Marble House, 1888-92

Royal residences have a melancholy all their own, which is probably due to the disproportion between their immensity and the tiny number of inhabitants, to their silence, which seems surprising after so many fanfares have been sounded there, and to their unchanging luxury, which proves by its antiquity the transience of dynasties, the inevitable impermanence of all things; and this emanation of the past, as overpowering and funereal as the scent of a mummy, affects even the simplest of mind.

Sentimental Education, *Gustave Flaubert*

Build me the finest summer "cottage" that money can buy, demanded William K. Vanderbilt of Richard Morris Hunt. The result, Marble House on Bellevue Avenue, is surely the built proof of Thorstein Veblen's theory of conspicuous consumption. Alva Vanderbilt, William's wife, was determined to be accepted into society; Mrs. Astor was determined to bar her. The Vanderbilt's solution was to buy their way in. Having constructed their palatial townhouse on Fifth Avenue in New York, also designed by Hunt, they focused on Newport for their next coup. Hunt was an appropriate employee, for despite his fine taste and training, it is recorded that he once pointed out to his son, "It's your client's money you're spending. Your business is to get the best results you can, following their wishes. If they want you to build a house upside down, standing on its chimney, it's up to you to do it and still get the best possible result."

Though Newport was growing accustomed to the larger and grander houses erected by the robber barons vying with one another for pre-eminence, the secrecy that veiled the building of Marble House excited all but the most world-weary. The ocean-front site was fenced off for four years, and 300 French and Italian workers were employed to build, build, build. Their foreign tongues were supposed to prevent details of the construction from being bandied about town.

Marble House was built as a thirty-ninth birthday present for Alva. She wanted a token of her husband's love equal to that of the Indian ruler, Shah Jahan, who had erected the Taj Mahal in memory of his wife at a cost of nine million dollars. Alva's blank check was eventually cashed for eleven million dollars; two million for the building and nine million for the decoration and the furniture.

Like her idol Louis XIV, the "Sun King," Alva was stricken with *la manie de batir,* the fever to build. Hunt created a melange of the Washington White House portico and the elevation of the Petit Trianon at Versailles. It was an expression of the Victorian mania for ostentation. The interior was created from the plunder of great European buildings combined with the very best contemporary craftsmanship available. The first splendor was the ten-ton bronze, steel, and crystal *grillage* that barred entry, a copy of the original in Versailles, which was embellished with an interwoven *W* and *V,* in imitation of the "Sun King's" monogram. White Tuckahoe marble covered the outer building, while the entrance hall and staircase were built of Siena marble, and the dining room, of pink Numidian marble. To store all this imported marble during construction, together with the bronzes, sconces, slate, iron, glass, chandeliers, paintings, tapestries, and furniture, a two-year lease was taken on numerous warehouses along the harbor wharf.

A pastiche of every major decorative order appears in the house, confusing visitors as they move from a Louis XIV-style ballroom covered in 23-carat gold leaf, the ceiling decorated with a school-of-Tintoretto painting, through a Gothic-revival drawing room decorated with velvet wall hangings repeatedly displaying the Vanderbilt oak-leaf-and-acorn crest (symbolizing strength and longevity), through a rococo-inspired library, and finally back to a Louis XIV-style dining room. On the second floor a similar inconsistency reigns: baronial/Jacobean here, Louis XV there. Amid the confusion and ostentation, comedy stole a laugh. For example, above the stair landing, the Vanderbilts, well-pleased with his work, permitted Hunt to insert a commemorative roundel depicting his own profile opposite that of Jules Hardouin-Mansart, architect to the "Sun King." The chairs in the dining room were made of solid bronze, and a footman was required behind each chair to help guests take their seats at dinners. In the early eighteenth century, Josiah Wedgwood had noted in his letters to his partner that while the aristocracy would relish the nudity of their classical Grecian figures, such anatomy would have to be veiled for the prim and censorious middle classes. At Marble House, most of the classical statues are indeed veiled.

Marble House did, however, contribute to Alva's greatest social success: She managed to get her reluctant daughter married off to a member of the English nobility—the ninth Duke of Marlborough—even if the marriage did end in divorce.

Above: *The stairs, floor, and walls of the main entry hall are paved and faced with yellow Siena marble.*

Opposite: *The front entrance is screened by a ten-ton steel and bronze doorway grille.*

Opposite: *As the setting for lavish balls, the Gold Ballroom may well have set the decorative standard for the Gilded Age.*

Above: *Perched atop the marble mantelpiece are bronze figures of Old Age and Youth holding candelabras.*

Above: *A portrait of Louis XIV by Pierre Mignard hangs over the fireplace.*

Opposite: *The dining room, designed with Allard et Fils of Paris, was based on the Salon of Hercules at Versailles.*

Opposite: *The Gothic Room displays Mr. Vanderbilt's medieval miniatures and Renaissance art objects.*

Above: *Gothic details such as carved panels with inset bas-relief figures, niches, and finials comprise the chimney breast.*

The Chinese Teahouse, 1912-14

Opposite: *The teahouse is a pastiche of Chinese design elements and Western post-and-beam construction techniques.*

There was a table set out under a tree in the front of the house, and the March Hare and the Hatter were having tea at it: a Dormouse was sitting between them, fast asleep, and the other two were using it as a cushion, resting their elbows on it, and talking over its head. "Very uncomfortable for the Dormouse," thought Alice; "only as it's asleep, I suppose it doesn't mind."
Alice's Adventures in Wonderland, *Lewis Carroll*

Alva Belmont, the former Mrs. William K. Vanderbilt, wanted a Chinese teahouse to perch at the end of her garden at Marble House (p. 148). She instructed Richard Hunt, Jr., the son of Richard Morris Hunt, to submit some sketches, for he had traveled in the Far East at her request. Hunt presented a number of drawings on Chinese-style silk scrolls painted in fine watercolors. Mrs. Belmont chose the most elaborate of schemes, with the greatest number of animal figures on the roof.

The interior was varnished to imitate lacquer and decorated with calligraphy and magnificent decorative moldings. The china for the teahouse was also designed by Hunt and decorated with Ming Dynasty figures which the architect had recorded while traveling through China. On completion of the teahouse, however, a major problem became evident: There was no place to make tea. The solution was a single-track railway that wound down through the ornamental gardens from the kitchens at Marble House. On a little railcar perched a liveried footman, balancing a silver tea tray. All was prepared for the opening ceremony, a Chinese party held one July evening in 1914. Mrs. Belmont, dressed in an ancient Chinese robe embedded with diamonds and pearls, received her guests to display her latest folly, which was bathed in the light of fluttering silk Chinese flags and bronze lanterns.

The teahouse completed, Mrs. Belmont embraced a new cause: women's suffrage. She proclaimed her newfound belief as bombastically as she had once trumpeted her social success: the marriage of her daughter to an English aristocrat. The teahouse was to become the setting for her Rights for Women meetings, at which the assembled drank from teacups inscribed "Votes for Women." She was to take up her new cause with vigor, galvanizing her followers into action, including one wilting suffragette whom she instructed, "Brace up, my dear. Just pray to God. *She* will help you."

Above: *Green-glazed terra-cotta roof tiles, hand-hammered copper dragons, and serpent-fish occupy the roof ridge.*

Opposite: *Wooden pilasters are painted with Chinese proverbs in calligraphic characters to imitate hanging scrolls.*

Above: *A bracketed chimney rises above the encrusted limestone cornice, anchored at the corner by a scroll-framed cartouche.*

Opposite: *The loggias that connect the two main wings were furnished with wicker during the summer months.*

Opposite: *The South Parterre Garden extends beyond the covered peristyle of paired columns.*

Above: *The gates contain the monogram C. V. and the acorn-and-oak-leaf family symbol.*

Above: *Massive bronze chandeliers hang in the Great Hall below the elaborate gilt cornice and painted sky ceiling.*

Opposite: *The Great Hall is lined with French Caen stone and rare Italian marbles.*

Belcourt Castle, 1892

Opposite: *Belcourt Castle was conceived by Richard Morris Hunt to resemble the Louis XIII hunting lodge at Versailles.*

High, sinister walls, like the walls of wharves, of dungeons for the damned, lifted into the watery air or swept in prodigious arcs of ruthless stone. Lost in the flying clouds the craggy summits of Gormenghast were wild and straining hair—the hanks of the drenched rock-weed. Buttresses and outcrops of unrecognizable masonry loomed over Steerpike's head like the hulks of mouldering ships, or stranded monsters whose streaming mouths and brows were the sardonic work of a thousand tempests. Roof after roof of every gradient rose or slid away before his eyes.
Gormenghast, *Mervyn Peake*

Designed for a bachelor, Oliver H. P. Belmont, Richard Morris Hunt's fifty-two-room castle was based on Louis XIII's hunting lodge at Versailles and was constructed, at the owner's request, to house his horses in the same magnificence that he himself enjoyed. In fact, one visitor remarked that it was "a palatial stable with an incidental apartment and an incidental ballroom"! Belmont also insisted that the layout should cater to his wish to ride his horses or drive his carriage right into the castle. As he could not bear to have his horses housed under another roof, the ground floor of the building consisted of one huge stable, each stall marked with a gold nameplate. The occupant of each stall was bedded down in pure Irish linen sheets embroidered with the Belmont crest.

This equestrian obsession did not confine itself to the ground floor. In the baronial hall upstairs, Belmont's two favorite horses were stuffed, mounted with mannequins, and dressed in some of his fine collection of ancient armor. The gloomy light shone through stained-glass windows depicting medieval tournaments. Belcourt was truly a *Boy's Own* fantasy until the feminine influence invaded in the persuasive form of Alva, William K. Vanderbilt's estranged wife. On marrying Belmont, Alva moved across the street to exert her social power mongering.

Under Alva's direction, entertainment became a theatrical extravagance. For formal dinners and balls, liveried footmen were placed on every sixth step of the grand staircase, each holding a gold candelabra. Those footmen, who were prepared to powder their own hair rather than wear wigs, were paid an extra five dollars, twice their weekly salary. The grand staircase, which took three years to carve out of oak, was a copy of the one in the Cluny Museum, Paris.

The ballroom is the most straightforwardly Gothic interior in the house, set with pointed windows, arches, and a high pointed vault, while the master bedroom, containing the first indoor shower in Newport, features walls hung with buttoned silk damask. The success of the interior's Gothic elements is determined by their witty theatricality.

Above: *A full-scale replica of an eighteenth-century Portuguese coronation coach is finished with 24-karat gold leaf.*

Opposite: *The Italian Banquet Hall is lit by a hand-cut crystal Russian imperial crown chandelier.*

Above: *The Grand Hall is decorated with French silk damask and carved oak paneling to reflect the Francis I style.*

Opposite: *The private chapel is illuminated by a wrought-iron and copper French Renaissance chandelier.*

Above: *The English Library features Gothic-style linenfold oak paneling and a sculpted mantelpiece finished in scagliola.*

Opposite: *The Maharajah of Jaipur's bed, in the master bedroom, is carved of teakwood.*

Above: *Thirteenth-century French glass was used in the tracery of the Gothic ballroom's windows.*

Opposite: *The armor collection stands in front of an English Mortlake wall tapestry.*

The Elms, 1899-1902

"Manor House."
"Is that the name of the house, Miss?"
"One of its names, boy."
"It has more than one, Miss?"
"One more. Its other name was Satis; which is Greek, or Latin, or Hebrew, or all three—or all one to me—for enough."
"Enough house!" said I; "that's a curious name, Miss."
"Yes," she replied; "but it meant more than it said. It meant, when it was given, that whoever had this house, could want nothing else."
Great Expectations, *Charles Dickens*

The Elms was built by a truly self-made man, Edward Julias Berwind. The son of an immigrant German cabinetmaker, Berwind joined the navy before establishing, with his brother, the family coal company, Berwind White Coal Mining, in Philadelphia. By the turn of the century, he was owner of the largest coal properties in the United States; his holdings included 90,000 acres in Pennsylvania, 90,000 in West Virginia, and 80,000 in Kentucky. He also held a lucrative contract to supply the American Navy with coal.

Hermionie Strawbridge Torrey, the daughter of a diplomat, became his wife in 1887 and, as her family had summered in Newport, they decided to buy a "cottage" called The Elms. In 1899, having purchased the adjoining land, they set about building a new summer "cottage." Horace Trumbauer, a relatively unknown architect from Philadelphia, was chosen. His specialty was the creation of loyal renditions of classical eighteenth-century French architecture. Curiously, however, Trumbauer had never even been to France and was consequently considered a mere copyist by his fellow professionals. How, they asked, could he possibly hope to create inspired interpolations of grand European palaces if he had never seen the originals? Since Richard Morris Hunt and Stanford White had both studied in Europe and were well versed in European aesthetics, it was widely felt that either would have been a better choice for architect.

Nevertheless, Trumbauer's house, an interpretation of the Château d'Agnès at Asnières, was considered both a faithful and well-constructed offering. In the best Newport tradition, it was built and furnished as a complete entity, at a final cost of one-and-a-half million dollars.

The house was only used by Berwind on weekends, for he would travel to his New York office every day.

Though he had made his fortune in coal, he was loathe to let his guests see it arriving into the house. For this reason, he had a tunnel built, in which coal cars ran on tracks, bringing the fuel in from a side street. Since there was no electricity available in Newport at that time, he also installed a coal-fed generator to supply the house with electricity.

The stairs at The Elms are particularly magnificent, built from Carrara marble so durable that even after nearly a century of plodding feet, including the more recent crowds of sightseers that stalk the house, it is not even slightly marked. It still looks as smooth and creamy as an untouched mozzarella cheese.

All the fireplaces in the house were also made of marble, as was the fashion, save for the one in the library, which was carved in wood and designed to hold copy of the *Madonna and Child* relief by the Italian Renaissance sculptor Giovanni della Robbia.

Mrs. Berwind was apparently quite a tyrant. An indicative example of her exacting ways was that she attached a timer to her staff bell, so that she could see how long the staff took to answer her.

Opposite: *The identical arched doorways could accommodate three carriages simultaneously.*

Above: *A bronze cherub romps on the back of a marble sphinx at the side of the front entry.*

Above: *The tripartite arcade of the entry hall is carried by double Ionic columns made from Italian Breccia marble.*

Opposite: *A gilt mirror reflects the white stucco relief decorations of the Louis XV-style ballroom.*

Above: *Classical symmetry is maintained in the Louis XVI-style salon designed by Allard et Fils of Paris.*

Above: *In the salon, musical instruments and farming motifs are represented in the carved wood grisaille lunettes.*

Above: *Eighteenth-century chinoiserie style pervades the Chinese Breakfast Room.*

Opposite: *Two oversized Venetian murals from the Palazzo Cornaro were the inspiration for the dining room.*

Opposite: *The conservatory is dominated by a white marble urn, given to the Berwinds as a housewarming gift.*

Above: *The Rouge Red marble fountain is decorated with bronze sea horses, dolphins, tritons, and a sea nymph.*

Opposite: *The west garden façade is a replica of Mansart's Château d'Agnes at Asnières outside Paris.*

Above: *The balustraded garden terrace provides a classical base for the Berwinds' extensive sculpture collection.*

Above: *Cast in 1830 by Pio Fede, the bronze statue of* Le Furie de Atamante *dominates the upper terrace.*

Opposite: *Formal parterre gardens lie hidden beyond the expansive lawn and to the right of the gazebo.*

Opposite: *A marble gazebo, designed in the eighteenth-century French Regency style, is clad with a patinated copper roof.*

Above: A Tigress with Cubs *was sculpted by Allard et fils of Paris.*

Above: *A marble and bronze fountain stands before the rusticated and arched wall that connects the stables.*

Opposite: *The garden statue of a winged goddess clutching a torch is dramatically set against the garden greenery.*

Rosecliff, 1901-02

Opposite: *The Grand Trianon at Versailles was the inspiration for the design of Rosecliff.*

We walked through a hallway into a bright rosy-colored space, fragilely-bound into the house by French windows at either end. The windows were ajar and gleaming white against the fresh grass outside that seemed to grow a little way into the house. A breeze blew through the room, blew the curtains in at one end and out the other like pale flags, twisting them up toward the frosted wedding-cake of a ceiling, and then rippled over the wine-colored rug, making a shadow on it as the wind does on the sea.

The Great Gatsby, *F. Scott Fitzgerald*

Rosecliff, a very feminine house, was built for Tessie and Herman Oelrichs by Stanford White. It is an alluring interpretation of the central portion of the Grand Trianon at Versailles and houses twenty-two bedrooms with accompanying bathrooms; all the major family bedrooms face the sea over the Cliff Walk.
Wherever you go in this white-glazed terracotta summer house, you must pass through the ballroom. The quest for summer is satisfied in this magnificent, airy room, the largest ballroom in Newport, measuring forty by eighty feet.
Following the demise of Mrs. Astor, the Queen of Newport society, three hostesses jointly assumed her title: Mrs. Oelrichs, Mrs. Belmont, and Mrs. Stuyvesant Fish. Mrs. Oelrich's concern with the upkeep of her household, and her desire to maintain a certain standard of entertainment, bordered on the obsessive. Rising early, she would meticulously inspect every room in the mansion insisting that each bed be freshly made up each morning, whether it had been slept in or not. She was so particular about the sheen on her marble floors that if they did not sparkle to her satisfaction, she would get down on her knees and scrub them herself. She at least had the wit to recognize this foible, requesting that, "When I die, bury me with a cake of Sapolio in one hand and a scrubbing brush in the other. They are my symbols."
She was captivated by the color white, no doubt because of its association with cleanliness. One of her greatest parties, in fact, was the White Ball. Disappointed that her white marble balustrade did not overlook the harbor at the back of the house, she set upon an extravagant solution: Twelve full-size replicas of sailing ships with gleaming white hulls were erected to give the impression of a full white fleet waiting attendance in the harbor. By the end of her life, like many Newport society ladies, she lost her mind. Michàel Strange, a relation, recalls visiting this old lady: "She would wander, a fragile and still incredibly beautiful person, her raven hair with its deep wave gone snow-white, through the rooms of her immense marble copy of the Villa Trianon, reseating her guests over and over again, pressing them

to take another ice, one more glass of champagne."
One of the most notable features of Rosecliff is the heart-shaped limestone staircase, which became known as "the sweetheart's staircase." In 1941 Rosecliff was bought by the singer Gertrude Niessen, for a mere $21,000. She lived there all on her own until one winter when, leaving the house without a caretaker, she returned to find that she had left one of the baths running for several months. The rich Aubusson rugs and parquet floors were inches deep in ice. She sold the property to the J. Edgar Monroes of New Orleans, who summered for several years at Rosecliff. They, in turn, eventually presented the house to the Newport Preservation Society in 1971.

Above: *Rosecliff's garden court façade is marked by the ballroom's paired Ionic columns and arched French doors.*

Opposite: *The Caen stone heart-shaped staircase spills into the front entrance hall, which is paved with white marble.*

Opposite: *The largest ballroom in Newport is decorated in a light rococo manner.*

Above: *The ballroom's south-central niche, now occupied by a piano, once housed a large white pipe organ.*

Above: *The salon combines a neo-Gothic chimneypiece and rococo Corinthian pilasters with a neoclassical ceiling.*

Opposite: *The Louis XVI-style dining room's low wainscoting and wall moldings were designed to frame tapestries.*

Harold Carter Brown House, 1893

The reverence due to (tradition) increases from generation to generation. The tradition finally becomes holy and inspires awe.
Human, All Too Human, *Friedrich Wilhelm Nietsche*

As the year-round residence of Mr. and Mrs. John Slocum, this is one of the few houses in Newport that remains a home, lived in today in the formal style of the nineteenth century. Only Felix de Welden's residence, Beacon Rock, has a similarly elegant and inhabited air. Its manageable, rather than palatial, proportions have made the transition into the late twentieth century very well, and the house has not become a "white elephant." Unlike so many of its neighbors, it was not built to impress Newport society; the family has confidently held its position in the area for two centuries. Being diplomats and devoted to the Republican Party cause, the Slocums entertain often and lavishly in this beautiful setting, which lends charm and comfort to their soirées. Harold Brown, of the Brown University family, commissioned the house for his new bride, Georgette Wetmore Sherman, a member of another prominent Newport family. The building was designed by the local architect Dudley Newton in a Gothic revival style, and the resulting exterior was rather heavy and depressing. Consequently, Mr. Brown rejected Newton's interior designs and turned to the young Ogden Codman to add his inimitable French taste to the house. Great improvements were also made by the landscape architect, Frederick Law Olmsted, who laid out the drive and gardens.

The honeymoon couple had traveled extensively in France and amassed a great many French artifacts. To provide a suitable Empire setting, Codman designed furniture based on plates from Charles Percier and Pierre François Fontaines' *Recueil de Decorations Interieures* (Paris, 1801). The Empire style was fashionable in the early nineties because of a major exhibition in 1891 in Paris entitled "The Arts at the Beginning of the Century," which had left an impression on Harold Brown.

Codman's devotion to the task led him to make more than fifty watercolor drawings for the project to show the Browns. This earnest dedication prompted Edith Wharton to write to him, advising that it was one thing to please his clients but that " . . . one colored sketch of each room . . . should be sufficient, and would be so, I am sure."

Unlike many of its neighbors along Bellevue Avenue, the Brown house is quite private, its unpretentious exterior belying its fine interiors. The interior design and furniture have remained utterly unchanged for a century, save for the removal of the Empire-style French sofas in the drawing room, which were too uncomfortable and delicate to use.

The house passed to the Slocum family through Mrs. Slocum, who is a member of the Brown family, from her childless aunt, lending it a distinctly matriarchal atmosphere. A continuity of ownership is evident throughout the house. One passes from room to room tracing the family genealogy from portraits and sepia photographs of four generations set in silver frames.

The Slocums have continued to collect fine treasures, and this generation's literary bent led Mr. and Mrs. Slocum to travel through Europe after World War II in search of the archives, letters, and unpublished works of James Joyce. The recent biography of Joyce's wife, *Nora,* by Brenda Maddox, details the Slocums' passionate efforts to preserve this material for university collections.

Above: *Codman was hired to create the appropriate Empire-style interiors for the Brown's collection of Napoleonic furniture.*

Opposite: *The original painted decoration is preserved in the Empire-style dining room.*

Opposite: *An inlaid ivory chess table stands before one of the arched cabinets housing the extensive porcelain collection.*

Above: *Codman sketched every aspect of the interior, including the curtains and wall decorations.*

Above: *The mahogany French Stand with marble top and ormolu mounts was acquired by the Browns on a trip to Paris.*

Opposite: *The library's decoration was drawn from Percier and Fontaine's 1801 Recueil de Decorations Interieures.*

Wakehurst, 1882-84

There exist houses whose appearance weighs as heavily upon the spirits as the gloomiest cloister, the most dismal ruin, or the dreariest stretch of barren land. There, houses may combine the cloister's silence with the arid desolation of the waste and the sepulchral melancholy of ruins. Life makes so little stir in them that a stranger believes them to be uninhabited until he suddenly meets the cold and listless gaze of some motionless human being, whose face, austere as a monk's, peers from above the windowsill at the sound of a stranger's footfall.
Eugénie Grandet, *Honoré de Balzac*

There is a gentle melancholy about this gray stone house, wrinkled with lattice, one of the first overtly historical and palatial summer "cottages" in Newport. Perhaps it is a melancholy born of imitation, for the house is a copy of Wakehurst Hall, the Elizabethan manor house in Sussex, England. Wakehurst's first owner was J. J. Van Alen, a confirmed anglophile, who spent much of his life in his fifteenth-century English home, Rushton Hall. In 1882 he appointed the English architect, Charles E. Kempe, to build a replica of Wakehurst, assisted by the Newport architect Dudley Newton. Many of the interiors of this summer house were removed from ancient European homes. The entire dining room, including the ceiling, was taken from a house in Bruges, the drawing room is reputedly the only complete and original Adam room in America, and the "den" used to belong to Lady Fitzherbert's London residence. The very furniture refused to relinquish its English origins, for it was shipped out from Rushton Hall to Newport every season, where it bided its borrowed time for a few weeks before its return. The Jacobean staircase that Van Alen bought to embellish the hall of Wakehurst, however, was found to be riddled with woodworm and could not be transported. Instead, it was painstakingly copied and installed.

Charles Kempe was an ideal collaborator in this imitative game, for he was a specialist in period design. His particular talent was painting glass in the late-medieval style. Examples of this type of decorative glass are handsomely displayed in the numerous bay windows throughout the house, which are set with painted roundels depicting a variety of late medieval scenes.

Van Alen summered at Wakehurst between 1882 and 1923. When he died, his daughter, Mrs. Louis Bruguière, inherited the house, and she clung to the grandeur of the past until her death in 1968. She insisted on running it like a formal nineteenth-century house, aided by a staff of twenty-three. The dining room was lit solely by candles, no short evening dresses were tolerated, and the estate greenhouses were maintained to ensure fresh flowers every day.

Above: *Reflecting its Elizabethan precedent, Wakehurst has parapeted gable ends crowned by ball-topped pinnacles.*

Opposite: *Wakehurst was given to J. J. Van Alen by his father to console him after the death of his young wife.*

The Waves, 1927

Opposite: *The Waves emerges from the southern tip of Aquidneck Island, Land's End.*

" . . . wuthering being a significant provincial adjective, descriptive of the atmospheric tumult to which its station is exposed in stormy weather. Pure, bracing ventilation they must have up there at all times, indeed: one may guess the power of the north wind, blowing over the edge, by the excessive slant of a few stunted firs at the end of the house; and by a range of gaunt thorns all stretching their limbs one way, as if craving alms of the sun. Happily the architect had the foresight to build it strong: the narrow windows are deeply set in the wall . . .
Wuthering Heights, *Emily Brontë*

The Waves stands on a rocky outcrop overlooking the southern tip of Rhode Island. Bracing itself against the crashing and tearing waves, the house, a spreading U, like a great gray cape, shelters the inner courtyard from the driving Atlantic winds. Of all the Newport houses it is the one best integrated into its surroundings—a triumph of nature over the artifice of its neighbors. Its strong foundation spreads across the jagged terrain like the wide-reaching roots of a huge oak tree, resisting the elements and holding its spectacular ground.

John Russell Pope designed this house as his own summer residence. It is not a meticulous copy of a historic building but rather offers a modern synthesis of the English country style that flourished in the Cotswolds and the American vernacular resort style. Pope believed, according to his biographer Royal Cortissoz, that "tradition is not the master of the true artist but his servant, leaving him free to place his own stamp upon a given building."

John Russell Pope was one of the most important American architects to emerge from the Ecole des Beaux Arts in Paris. He was born in New York in 1874, the son of a portrait painter, and after a three-year course in architecture at Columbia, he spent two years in Italy at the American Academy in Rome, having won the McKim Roman Scholarship in 1897. He traveled extensively in Europe, particularly in Greece. Returning to America, he was heralded as a leading architect of his day. Pope was renowned for his monumental and grand style—he had studied many of the classical monuments in Europe—and was consequently commissioned to design some important ones for the American nation, including the War Memorial for American Troops of Montfaucon in France and the Theodore Roosevelt memorials in Washington and New York. He died in 1937 in New York, and the *London Times* recalled his achievements in its obituary:

"He confined his attentions to no one district, or any single style or form of architecture. His works followed one another in no seeming order: memorials, town halls, railway stations, churches, government buildings, museums, art galleries and private houses were built to his designs in all parts of the country."

Among his most acclaimed domestic works are the buildings at Yale University, the National Gallery of Art, the Jefferson Memorial, and residences for the Vanderbilt and Mills families. His works abroad include the Duveen Sculpture Galleries at the Tate Gallery in London, and the extensions to the British Museum.

The Waves was the first building in Newport to be converted into condominiums, in the 1950s. Sadly, the interiors, where Pope lived and worked, have consequently not survived.

Above: *An undulating slate roof hugs the windswept site of The Waves.*

Above: *Pope's half-timbered studio collects soft northern light through the broad expanses of leaded-glass windows.*

Following pages: *The multiple-shafted brick-Tudor-style chimneys rise from the horizontal, curving mass of the house.*

Bibliography

Amory, Cleveland. *The Last Resorts*. New York: Harper & Bros., 1952.

Baker, Paul R. *Richard Morris Hunt*. Cambridge: MIT Press, 1980.

Chase, David. "Notes on the Colonial Revival in Newport." *Newport History*, volume 55, Spring, 1982.

Cherol, John. "Richard Morris Hunt." *The Architectural Digest*, 1985.

Chyet, Stanley F. *Lopez of Newport, Colonial American Merchant Prince*. Detroit: Wayne State University Press, 1970.

Clark, Kenneth. *An Architectural Monograph of Newport*, volume 8, No. 3. New York: White Pine Monograph Series, June 1922.

Cortissoz, Royal. *The Architecture of John Russell Pope*, Volumes I, II, III. New York: William Helburn, 1924–30.

Downing, Antoinette and Scully, Vincent. *The Architectural Heritage of Newport, Rhode Island, 1640–1915*. Cambridge: Harvard University Press, 1952.

Elliott, Maud Howe. *This Was My Newport*. Cambridge: Mythology Co., 1944.

James, Henry. *Portrait of Places*. Boston: J. R. Osgood & Co., 1883.

James, Henry. *The American Scene*. New York: Harper & Bros., 1907.

La Farge, C. G. "Give Me Rhode Island." *House & Garden*, July, 1949.

Mason, G. C. *Newport and its Cottages*. Boston: J. B. Osgood & Co., 1875.

Mason, G. C. *Newport and its Environs*. Newport: C. E. Hammett, Jr., 1848.

Metcalf, P. C. "The Interiors of Ogden Codman Junior in Newport." *Antiques*, September, 1980.

Morris, C. "Newport, the Maligned". *Everybody's*. Vol. 19, September, 1908.

Sherwood, Mary Elizabeth Wilson. "Newport Villas." *Art Journal*. The Homes of America, Series 6, October, 1876.

Stern, Robert A. M. *Pride of Place, Building the American Dream*. New York: Houghton Mifflin, 1986.

Thomas, Harriet E. *Old Homes with Histories*. Newport: Remington Ward, 1928.

Van Rensselaer, Mrs. J. K. *Newport, Our Social Capital*. Philadelphia: J. B. Lippincott Co., 1905.